Finding Harmony

Finding Harmony

—◄o►—

MATTHEW DEL NEVO

WIPF & STOCK · Eugene, Oregon

FINDING HARMONY

Wipf & Stock
An Imprint of Wipf and Stock Publishers
199 W. 8th Ave., Suite 3
Eugene, OR 97401

www.wipfandstock.com

PAPERBACK ISBN: 978-1-5326-3307-2
HARDCOVER ISBN: 978-1-5326-3309-6
EBOOK ISBN: 978-1-5326-3308-9

Manufactured in the U.S.A.   DECEMBER 20, 2017

Nothing, neither in nature nor in life, exists in isolation; everything has its foundation in an endless relationship with everything else, including all that is willfully arbitrary, unnecessary, harmful.

RICHARD WAGNER[1]

There can be no objective rules of taste which would, by means of concepts, determine what is beautiful. For every judgement from this source is aesthetic; i.e. a feeling of the subject. And there is no concept of an object which is the ground of its determination. To seek a principle of taste which would indicate the general criterion of the beautiful in terms of specific concepts is a fruitless endeavor, because what is sought is impossible and self-contradictory.

IMMANUEL KANT[2]

I don't adhere to rabbis, preachers, evangelists, all of that. I've learned more from the songs than I've learned from any of this kind of entity. The songs are my lexicon. I believe the songs.

BOB DYLAN[3]

1. Wagner, *Artwork of the Future*, 17.
2. Kant, *Critique of Judgment*, 79.
3. David Gates, "Dylan Revisited," *Newsweek*, October 6, 1997.

Contents

Introduction

THIS IS A PHILOSOPHY book—a philosophy for readers of self-help books or for those who do not like self-help books very much but are not quite certain why or if they are wrong not to do so. Today self-help books come in a multitude of guises (religious, managerial, business, education) and, in every area of life and livelihood, "positive thinking" and behavioral correction is enjoined or encouraged. In Christian circles the positivistic self-help ethos extends into "spirituality" and spiritual reading and practices, for example, "the purpose-driven" life or church, all backed up by the Bible, ostensibly. The difference between self-help and spirituality is blurred. This book examines the blur.

This book does not give a recipe for finding harmony, nor does the author think harmony is to be found at large any time soon, but this book *does* provide a stimulus for thinking in harmonious terms about things—about ourselves and our time—which is to say it is about thinking in terms of soul and the feeling of soulfulness, and the recognition of soulfulness and its obverse, the evacuation or voiding of soul: soullessness. The connection between harmony and soul and soulfulness is one the book makes.

Here, though, let me add that soullessness is not the same as meaninglessness. Many so-called "religious" types have spoken of our times as meaningless or nihilistic (governed by no higher values and tending nowhere). To the contrary, I think our times are as meaningful as every time, if not *actually more so*. Our times are not static; something is afoot. I discuss the eponymous "signs of the times" in one part of the book, and in another I discuss the song as a principal instance of where soul is restored today in a generally soulless age. Song, I think, is a principal sign of our times.

Since Aristotle, well before Christianity, the soul has been understood as the active principle of life. At the level of our human being, soul is vital force. The fact that today we have biochemical explanations for life allows us to forget about soul. But soul has a meaning at the *psychological* level, its own level, as *psyche* means "soul." Since Freud, who rediscovered soul through his studies of dreams, everyday life, and jokes, at the start of the twentieth century, philosophy has needed to get more psychological if it is to stay human—something philosophy (along with technological sciences) has not been managing to do. At the questioning and questing level of reflection, then, soul—should we wish to give it a rough definition at the start—is *the unison of our inner sensibilities and sensitivity*. By way of a quick explanation: inwardly we can never be a unity, we cannot be "centered" or "balanced" except in a very loose metaphorical sense, perhaps, but the different parts of ourselves can work together and, as it were, sing in unison—like the different cells of our bodies all do at the unconscious, physical level. Sensibility is a unison of our mind and our emotions in experience; to have a "sensibility" for something indicates an understanding, but not merely a cognitive understanding. Colloquially we would say a "deeper" understanding. Empathy is an example of sensibility. Empathy is more than a cognition on one hand but not "just a feeling" on the other. Melancholy and joy are linked sensibilities. We use our sensibility to understand and enjoy life more. Soullessness refers to the loss or absence of soul in this regard.

Soul bridges into spirituality. St. Francis de Sales rightly said: "our spiritual lives are what love's activity makes them: a heart devoid of emotion is devoid of love."[1] Love is the most overpowering sensibility. Jesus' instruction to love your neighbor as yourself stops love from destroying the peace that is natural and good and helps prevent us from destroying ourselves and peace at large with our passions and delusions. Soul personified as the young girl in mythology has always been waiting for love and in love with love. Love's arrow will impregnate her and bring new life to birth. Love is the principle of creativity and inspiration and relates to sensibility in this regard.

This book is written so that anyone, whether religious or not religious, may read it. Harmony is universal, and so are the signs of the times I refer to in the book, and so is the song.

Harmony is a value from music. Harmony has to do with health and well-being too. Harmony is something religion has yet to learn in the age of world religions, because religion yesterday and today—contrary to the words of the founders of said religions (whoever they may be)—is marked, most often, not by unity and understanding and compassion, but by ignorance, exclusivism, sectarianism, religious conflict, and so forth. This book is a modest contribution to finding harmony in the teeth of bad religion and ideology, a contribution that works only with a sense of humanity.

The harmony is never complete. The harmony eventuates in the performance. It begins in the composition.

1. François de Sales, *L'amour de Dieu*, VII, 7.

3

Previously I have written about soul and soulfulness.[2] This condensed book follows from the earlier books. The song remains the same.

2. Del Nevo, *Art Music*, *Valley Way of Soul*, and *Work of Enchantment*. Full details are in the bibliography.

Chapter 1

Harmonizing Personality, Soul, and Spirit

FROM SOUL

B ODY, SOUL, AND SPIRIT is a division we get from the New Testament. It is Christian thinking. In his First Letter to the Thessalonians, Paul says, "May your whole spirit, soul and body be kept blameless until the coming of the Lord" (5:23). Jesus in Matthew 10:28 warns against those who kill the soul but not the body, again making the distinction. There are many such references to the distinction between body, soul, and spirit in the New Testament, indicating that these should not be confused. Paul says in Romans: "I do not understand what I do. For what I want to do I do not do, but what I hate, that I do. . . . for I have the desire to do what is good, but I cannot carry it out. For I do not do what I want to do, but the evil I do not want to do—this I keep on doing" (7:15–19). We all know this inner conflict, sometimes quite excruciatingly, sometimes to the detriment of everything in our lives.

Body and soul is a pre-Christian divide we find in Plato and Aristotle. For Plato the soul preexists. That

means, when born, we are loaded with stuff; we are prepro-
grammed, so to speak, and we live our life in terms of these
predispositions—what in the East they call past-life karma.
And we leave life—or are supposed to leave it—richer. And
the soul moves on, incarnating through many cycles (generations) in different bodies. This is not to be taken literally,
I suppose, but as a metaphor for the richness of time and
human being (culture) as time goes on. In Aristotle the pic-
ture is not so clear. Soul and body are like the harmony and
the lyre. When the instrument breaks, the harmony disap-
pears too. Aristotle's emphasis was more on the material
and changing, Plato's on the immaterial (soul) and cyclical.

New Age schools often have diagrams of "man"—
quite complicated ones. For example, the Orphic theogony
(see fig. 1).

Orpheus

CHART OF THE ORPHIC THEOGONY

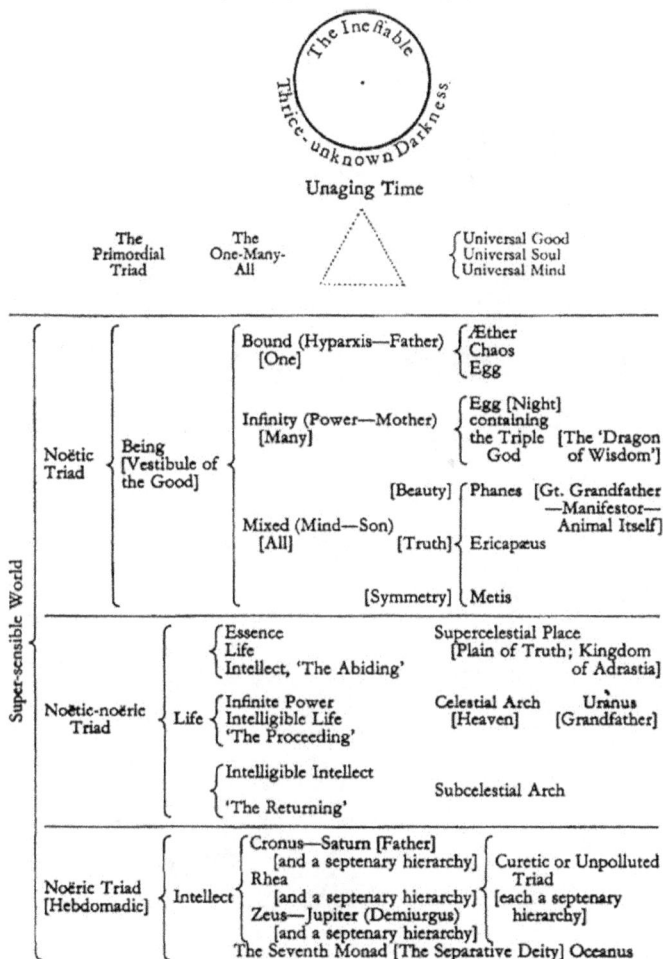

The Ineffable

Thrice-unknown Darkness

Unaging Time

| The Primordial Triad | The One-Many-All | △ | Universal Good
Universal Soul
Universal Mind |

Super-sensible World	Noëtic Triad	Being [Vestibule of the Good]	Bound (Hyparxis—Father) [One]		Æther Chaos Egg
			Infinity (Power—Mother) [Many]		Egg [Night] containing the Triple God [The 'Dragon of Wisdom'] God
			Mixed (Mind—Son) [All]	[Beauty] [Truth] [Symmetry]	Phanes [Gt. Grandfather—Manifestor—Animal Itself] Ericapæus Metis
	Noëtic-noëric Triad	Life	Essence Life Intellect, 'The Abiding'		Supercelestial Place [Plain of Truth; Kingdom of Adrastia]
			Infinite Power Intelligible Life 'The Proceeding'		Celestial Arch [Heaven] Uranus [Grandfather]
			Intelligible Intellect 'The Returning'		Subcelestial Arch
	Noëric Triad [Hebdomadic]	Intellect	Cronus—Saturn [Father] [and a septenary hierarchy] Rhea [and a septenary hierarchy] Zeus—Jupiter (Demiurgus) [and a septenary hierarchy] The Seventh Monad [The Separative Deity] Oceanus		Curetic or Unpolluted Triad [each a septenary hierarchy]

Figure 1. The Orphic theogony.[1]

1. *Rosicrucian Digest* 86, no. 1 (2008) 6–7, https://6e1cf6feb01b b13df8b28eefe63bc367089bf5080f150aeb98c7.ssl.cf5.rackcdn.com/ Online_Digest_Orphic_Full_2008-04-18.pdf.

Or consider the diagram drawn by Madam Blavatsky and shown by Alice A. Bailey and followed by Agni yoga, to mention but the central mainstay of New Age philosophy (see fig. 2).

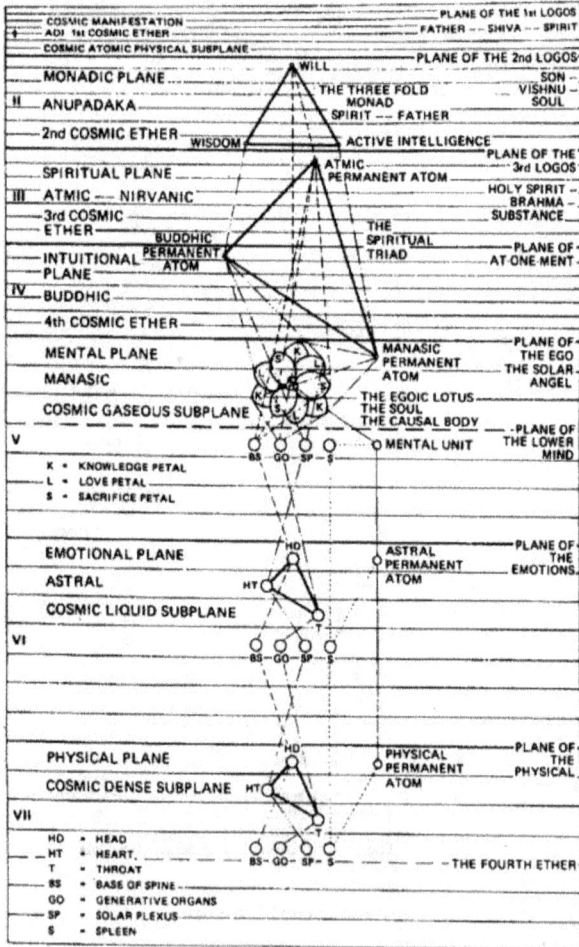

Figure 2. Diagram drawn by Madam Blavatsky.[2]

2. http://www.kheper.net/integral/planes.html.

Or—new but not New Age—from Freudian psychoanalysis, consider Lacan's diagram of desire (see fig. 3).

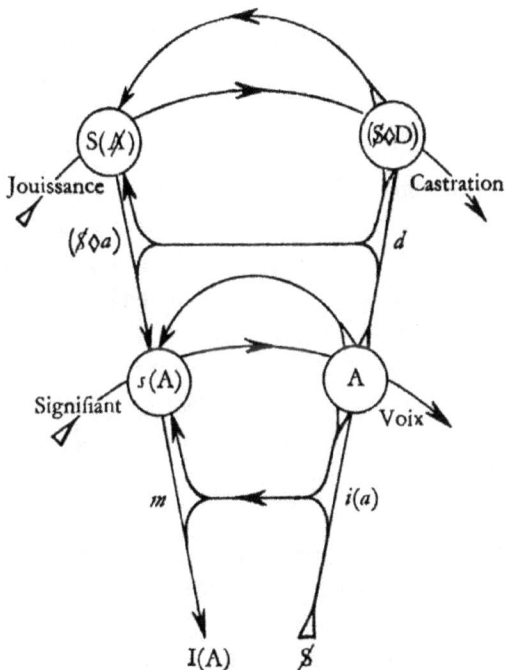

Figure 3. Lacan's diagram of desire.[3]

At different times on separate occasions I have explained these diagrams, but of what help are any such explanations or understandings? Ultimately they are a dead letter, useless. What they have in common is that they are extrinsic and impersonal, which weighs against our experience, which is intrinsic (to us) and so personal. But how

3. http://braungardt.trialectics.com/projects/psychoanalysis/lacans-life/graph-of-desire/

personally are we to take experience? Are we to clutch our experience close to our breast and claim "mine!"? Or are we to let it go? Does it depend on the specific experience? Then what is the rule?

Whatever the case, it is our experience that we operate on two levels: our force and our physique. Body and mind. Body and soul. Chakras below the navel and above the navel—or however we want to describe it. Often we see the difference between levels only with the wisdom of hindsight; often our higher level—our soul level—is blocked. What is called "thinking" (I mean the running mind, running like a tap) drowns out soul—because thinking belongs to mind and mind belongs to body, essentially. Body and mind are one. The personality associated with body and mind has its concerns in the here and now, while the soul has concerns that tend to wait in the wings until they can get on stage—when the personality fails. Usually this is when we fall into serious difficulties or troubles.

Personality is how we come across, how we show ourselves. It is keyed to our social self.

Soul is keyed to our destiny—to becoming all that we are (Nietzsche). The trouble here is we do not know what we are capable of. Sometimes other people and circumstances and trauma hold us in thrall and we never become all that we were meant to be.

Destiny is not fate but is to do with our flourishing. Destiny depends on God in the Jewish sense, the monotheistic sense. We are alive and here and we ask ourselves, why? Why am I here? What is the point of it? The world is a wondrous spectacle. Everything is connected. We feel there is a reason for our being here, there is a purpose, but we are not sure what. We need to find out. We may feel too that the world is not just "there" either, that it too is like a creation because of its beauty and the interconnectedness of everything; yet God is, but we don't know who God is and need to find out.

God is associated with spirit—with the Holy Spirit, in Christianity; with Absolute Spirit, in Hegel. The spirit searches us out: "the spirit searches all things even the deep things of God" (1 Cor 2:10). This is where Western religion and the Western sense of God are quite different from the Eastern. In the West the spirit searches *us* out. There *is* spirit. This disallows immobility and stasis as a pure way—zazen or singular mindfulness. The West is driven, it is restless (Augustine). The spirit in the West is not dormant, not nothing, not an idea or psychological; it is metaphysical (uncontained) and yet active. Jesus wandered. He was homeless and said so. Paul was homeless. They all were. When it came to be that all roads lead to Rome, Christian religion was ripe for reformation, for a decentering, which is what happened. Jesus is not at the center of Christian religion: he is on the road with it. That is the road that retrospectively we recognize as history. History is an invention of the West. For history is cultural—it is produced—nor is it simply natural to think historically.

The whole Bible testifies to this fact that spirit searches us out. We cannot find the spirit: we have to *let the spirit find us*. God finds the prophets and they say, "Who are you, Lord?" And God presses them into *action that will disrupt the status quo* and change society. Leave your father, your origins, your heritage, your homeland, and get away to a land that I will show you, God tells Abraham (cf. Gen 12:1). Biblical religion is creative, not cosmic. The creative is about making something be that is not already—not a fantasy image of what supposedly is. Creation over cosmos, command over order, disruption over balance: that is what the Bible teaches. But the New Testament has no revelation on human or divine creativity (Berdyaev): it is lacking. Yet it is what we need today. Jews and Christians will say "we are co-creators" with God, but what does that mean? It can be a way of giving divine legitimation to our self-interest or business interests—always a problem in Christianity, with its colonizing tendency.

In the Bible God is in search of man (Heschel). This means we are not just *here*. We are here *with a purpose*. As if we have been "put" here. We are here to *be* something and *do* something. But what? This is the sense we have in the West of *vocation*. We are taught to discern our vocation—what it is we are meant to be. We have to discover our vocation by trial and error. These things, destiny, vocation, are in the spirit. Our personality will be formed by them. They manifest from within to without, they are not in and of themselves social.

In this Western culture of which the Bible is the foundational writing, spirit is not neutral: it is *personal*. This is how Western culture developed personality and personhood in the first place. Personality is not natural either—any more than history is—it is cultural, it is produced. *Character* is natural. Personality is the cultivation of character, which is like the default. America today is the denouement of this development of personality. In America many people have reached the end of the possibility of personality development and wonder, what next? So they get into spirituality movements and such like, or drugs and distractions, or go wild. The personality is what in esotericism is called the Dweller on the Threshold; crossing the threshold comes next. "And after this our exile," wrote T. S. Eliot, in the poem "Ash Wednesday" (1930). He knew what we are talking about. Eliot saw Western culture itself on that threshold, a threshold he personally crossed ("because I do not hope to turn again"). The other option, rather than to cross the threshold into soul realization, is regression. That is the step European culture took in 1939. The world is still trying to find its way back, but it might be too late.

We must differentiate personality from soul, and self from soul. The personality is the self. The self is what we *say* we are. The soul, by contrast, is *what in fact we are*, but do not *know* that we are—do not know *yet*. In time we may know. Soul works *through* personality, if personality is attuned to it. Just as Blake said, we do not hear *with* our senses, but *through* our senses. The soul works the other way round, externalizing in the senses, where it is inwardly sensed to begin with. The senses are the chief inlets of soul in our age, Blake said. They are also the chief outlets: the way we see, touch, smell, listen, taste, and think give out soul if they are empathetic, sympathetic, compassionate, imaginative, open. It is from a soul sense, not a sense of self (selfish) personality base, that we do *spiritual work*. This has to do mainly—and this is how we recognize that it *is* spiritual—with awakening the inner senses. For many of us who do inner work of some kind—study, art, or yoga and meditation from the East—what we are doing is *attuning* ourselves to deeper (governing) patterns of being. "Sacred attunement," Michael Fishbane calls it, with reference to his own Jewish tradition. We attune to whence these traditions have come and the generations that have transmitted the practices down to where we are now; but we attune as well to our generation, for *soul is a group phenomenon*. Soul is never about me. Self is personal, but soul is pure empathy, pure attunement, so impersonal, generational. Soulwise, we attune to the time, we attune to inner work, for we understand the importance of inner work if we have a sense of soul. Whereas, if we work from a personality base only, then we work only outwardly, externally. Great souls (or "old" souls) also work outwardly, but from a deep well of the spirit within, externalizing itself. This is qualitatively different from external "good works" that lack this deep well, except perhaps in payment of lip service to it. So "good works" can be soulful or soulless.

Between what we *say* we are and what *in fact* we are is a gap—like a fault line. This gap is the unconscious (abbreviated by Freud thus: *ucs*). The *ucs* is not a realm; it is this gap between two levels of the conscious (*cs*).

There is *ucs* at each level, of personality and of soul. At the level of personality there is *ucs* because perception is always partial, perspectival, fragmentary; so we are *ucs* because we rely on perception for understanding. There is *ucs* at the level of the soul, because the soul is not a knower, but a reflector. Spirit refracts through the soul and the soul reflects spirit outward onto the material plane of being, where our senses are. It is *soul* that reflects God within, and shines out, so we say the soul "knows" God—"knowing" here being a metaphor. It is the self that knows. The self is cognitive, but the self in and of itself does not know God like "believers" say they do, because God is not a cognition. Soul knows God by reflection, not by cognition. That is why the soul is symbolized most often by the moon. The moon knows the sun by reflecting it to earth. We know God by reflecting the Most High through our soul into our day-to-day, our personality level, but we do not know God directly (literally) or reason about him. God language is symbolic if it is at all meaningful, and the symbolic register depends on levels of awareness. The personality in full bloom, as in, say, a Hollywood celebrity, is the Dweller on the Threshold the person on the brink of inner initiation and the start of a spiritual journey, a new age or stage of life. Many people need to work on their personality in our time. Then self-help can help. For big egos into spirituality the work can mean cutting through the deceit that we are more spiritual or advanced than in fact we are. This (what Chögyam Trungpa

called "spiritual materialism") is the great affliction of self-
help or personality work that it is held back or retarded by
the *illusion* of spirituality, confused often with religiosity.
The overall point I am making here is that *a person knows
spirit only insofar as he or she knows soul.* Spirituality work
can be soulless as well; as soulless as jogging at the gym in
the fake light, conditioned air, staring at a dashboard and
piping digitalized noise through the earbuds directly into
the head. But people do not notice the soulless anymore
after they become acclimatized to it, like men in jail who
after a while get used to the regime of the place and find
it easier to live inside than outside. One good thing about
religion generally (discounting Protestant religion) is that it
is inherently soulful, therefore it is better if "spirituality", if
that is what one is after, take place under religious auspices,
not outside them, if possible. But it is very often not possible in our time when religion itself is so dead. People are
getting into spirituality precisely to get away from religion,
to let the dead bury their dead. I appreciate this conundrum
and would only caution spiritual seekers to be soulful about
it. In any case I want to emphasize soul, not spirituality.
Fr. David Ranson has said: "Without religion spirituality
loses its depth, without spirituality religion becomes doc-
trinaire. If theology is faith seeking understanding, perhaps
spirituality is faith seeking experience."[4] And soulfulness in
either case lies close to a love for arts. Why I just discounted
Protestantism in such a cavalier and wholesale way just
now is because its very soullessness, its iconoclasm, by the
same token cuts "believers" free for themselves to create,
so from Bach, a great many creative giants were Protestant:
Beethoven, Hegel, Kant, Schopenhauer, Wagner, Nietzsche
and so on were all Protestants. America is a Protestant
foundation. It is the Protestant spirit that is innovative,

4. Ranson, *Across the Great Divide*, 32.

precisely because it so desperately seeks what it lacks, what it has lost and left behind: soul culture.

The soul does not *know*: it *reflects*. The soul is *not gnostic*: it is *drastic* (Jankélévitch). "Drastic," from the Greek *drasteon*, means something to be done; *drastikos* means effective, efficacious, even going to the extreme, as in "drastic measures." Redemption in Christianity is drastic, not gnostic. Someone is drowning and about to be swept away by the current and you pull them out—this is the idea. Faith is drastic, not gnostic, because it acts without knowing, but in trust or love. Music is drastic, as it operates directly on our inner sensibility. Unlike faith that lives in hope and may never bear fruit or may inadvertently lead to undesirable fruits (as Christianity has shown), music happens in *real time* right in our ears. Music is drastic in that, like action, like time, it is *irreversible*; therefore, it is unlike thought and knowledge. Music happens to the soul. Music is made soul to soul and to listen to it—as at a concert—we have to switch off our self. Music reaches into the expanse of the soul and explores the space from soul to soul. Music occupies the juncture of difference between I and Thou; that is why it brings people together. Music occupies space—the space in which it is played—but music is linear at the same time, it goes from start to finish. This spaciousness, this linearity is a feature of the soul; neither are physical, or even empirical. As music does not follow the time on the clock, it may transport one, or it may drag. Music follows soul time.

Time is a player in bodywork, soul work, self-development, and not just in the personal sense but within longer narratives. Body, soul, and spirit are not the same in every age. The body wears away and perishes. Personality changes over time and perishes with the body. It is not eternal. The soul has its ages too. We speak of "the soul of an age." The soul of the age of the Enlightenment, or of Victorian England, is not the soul of our age. We usually tell the soul of an age in its art and music. We speak as well of "the spirit of an age," by which we mean what back of it seems to drive it. The age of the Enlightenment was driven by a dream of establishing knowledge. The colonial age was driven by a sense of Christian mission to bring civilization to uncivilized places, a dream of the expansion of civilization—though perhaps it was hijacked by a desire for conquest and by greed (if these were not there to start with). The feudal age, like many traditional societies, was driven (if that is the word for a more static world) by a sense of the order of things and a sense of overarchingness, for which they had different words: God, sky, heavens. And the architecture of the great cathedrals reiterated this sense in stone.

We have a personal sense of soul, too, which is always *within* the soul of an age. Soul as a group phenomenon is generational, not first and foremost individual. The only real individuals are the untimely ones, who, by not fitting into their times, like Nietzsche, are generative for future sensibility and ideas, and what they generate may take centuries to digest. Aristotle is the prime example. His heyday was in the scholastic Middle Ages, around 1500 years after his death, out of which came his legacy (as advances on Aristotle were made) in the form of modern science and reason. Mostly, though, we are of our generation and our provenance. But everyone born and every personality that is allowed to develop (thanks to a culture like modern Western culture oriented to personality development) receives a touch of the soul that is not one's own. This touch is our inspiration and we usually recognize it outside us in what we are inspired by; the soul will leave us (our personality, bound to body and mind) one day, but we will leave behind the results of our actions and the love we shared. And all of this will take body in turn and be thought up and rethought and thought through by others. Yet, while we have time, our personality can do much for the soul. The personality does not need to wait on inspiration as in the olden days, but our personalities (that is, we ourselves) can create inspiration. We can be generative of inspiration if we are creative: like the founders of every lineage (founders of religion belong to another category, which we need not go into here). Creativity is the key, and that means, in the first place, tapping into our creativity, which means *anything*: we define our creativity by ourselves, by our practices, by their fruits; but of course it is not us—not I—but that greater force of inspiration or grace working in and through us; for this we lay down our lives; for this we die at the right time (Nietzsche). I am not merely referring to "being artistic," but, as Nietzsche said, to becoming all that you are. That means allowing to manifest all that you are within yourself, unknown to yourself when you start out. The only clues we have to begin with are what we call our "interests." Creativity goes from there. The revelation about human creative potential (and its destructive side effects when out of hand and "mad") is the revelation to come (Berdyaev). It is not in the New Testament. The inklings of it are given to our time, to the new age, and they start with German philosophy in Hegel's day (to pick a start date from my own world) but . . . they manifest more clearly in the *music* of that era than the ideas. Music led the way. *This is not a revelation of the word* (*logos*). We shall return to this in chapter 3.

Meanwhile, getting back to what I was saying, creativity is the link between soul and personality. Personality has the power of soul-making. And this is the point I want to make: soul-making is different from self-help on one hand and spirituality on the other. Self-help develops personality and helps the personality in the external world. Soul-making opens the inwardness of sensibility to states of receptivity to promptings of inspiration and the soul's search for divinity. Soul work is the groundwork of genuine spirituality and therefore genuine religion. Spirituality and religion can never afford to leave soul work behind or ignore it or factor it out. It does so at a fatal cost to its own interests and truth. By *truth* I mean knowing *what* something is and *why* it is. If we know the what and the why of something, we know the truth. Self-help only goes so far to help us before it becomes a hindrance, because soul works not through our self but through others, through the symbolic other (Lacan), through empathy, by the decentering of oneself (rather than centering), by taking the road less traveled (Robert Frost / M. Scott Peck)—this last being *absolutely native to all creativity*. Soul-making can be inner work (a spiritual practice) or outward work with and for others. Soul-making is double-sided.

Soul is less in our personality, our social self, than in our *sensibility*, indicated by our sensitivity—how we reflect others, events, and circumstances. The soul can extrovert into the personality and the world or introvert into character. But soul as sensibility in our time (which does not go for all time) is our *cultivated inwardness*; and this in the general sway, the dance to the music of time, is a movement of the spirit. The spirit moves in mysterious ways, eccentrically. I like James Hillman's idea that soul work is not about being centered, but about becoming eccentric. Find your eccentricity. This is what "know thyself" really means. Think how eccentric Socrates was. Trying hard to be centered or mindful can be actually soul-destroying and you never become who you were meant to be through it. The demonization of ego in Eastern-influenced spiritual psychology is a symptom of not knowing what to do with oneself. So I will try and get rid of ego. But we cannot go back to a pre-personal psychology. In fact our technological networked humanism is *already post-personal*. I shall enlarge on this is a moment.

What I am talking about now is the point at which soul work and spiritual religious practices get mixed up. My belief is that spiritual religious practices are for souls, and we need to do the soul work first. If you jump from the individual personality level—that is, self-help—to spiritual religious practices like meditation, you may go wrong, because you are missing out on the soul level. The soul is the level from which to embark on spiritual practices.

In traditional pre-personal culture, simple and pure people (characters) stay at the level of religious piety and superstition. For people of developed personality, such as those of Western culture or those who are influenced by it, that is, almost everyone, we need to be soulful before we get spiritual. If we aim to be soulful we may even find that by doing so we have become more spiritual without trying. This is because while we are doing soul work, in the background, the spirit is not dormant. *Trying* to be spiritual is a personality thing and always backfires because it misses the soul. Religion saves the soul, not the self. In Christianity they say you cannot get to heaven by trying to be good, but by grace. In Buddhism, nirvana is gained not by finding oneself, but by losing oneself, by "awakening" to what is and discovering the truth of *not I*. Samuel Beckett staged a marvelous theater piece having this title. He wrote it in 1972 for Billie Whitelaw and ran over the lines with her by phone from Paris, over and over in long-distance rehearsals. The stage is pitch black. All you can see is a white mouth, completely disembodied, and you hear speech in a continuous unbroken monologue, which ends in a famous scream of "I not I." Whitelaw gave one performance and had a nervous breakdown. The truth of not I is not easy. Go over the brink or wake up, it is a knife edge.

But a lot of the endemic depression and psychological distress in developed societies has to do with the cutting point, where the self fails the soul and fails itself as a result.

A TRANSITION TIME

I've said body, soul, and spirit are not the same in every age.

It is our age, not ages gone by, that isolates the human person and fragments him or her into bits. Think of all the specializations in body parts. Think of the doctor who sees you immobilized on a hospital bed as what you have got, as a thing within his specialization, not as a person, not a suffering soul. Nurses no longer sit by the bedside but at the console in the nurses' station. Person as screen digit, as bed number.

In fact we are traversed invisibly and inaudibly, yet manifestly, by economic, aesthetic, historical, political, religious, ancestral thought waves. We may pretend there are no such national or racial unifying rays and dismiss them on the basis of rationalism as "stereotypes," but humor knows better, because as Freud said they unloose the unconscious from the superego: there *are* stereotypes, like them or not, and we *do* act them out, in spite of ourselves. Buddhism calls this acting out *karma*. Karma also *produces* acting out: the turning of the wheel of life and death, repetition. The Bible calls karma "blood-guiltiness": stuff we inherit and pass on so that it is reborn or reincarnated, with us or "me" in it. So we are what Jean Baudrillard (d. 2007) calls "transparent." We are *shot through* like light through glass by what Baudrillard calls "transversals."

Baudrillard has been authoritatively called the most important philosopher of the turn of the millennium (J. G. Ballard). He is not alone in saying we live in an Age of Transparency (Daniel Barenboim has said it too) when, to use the phrase of Marx, all that is solid melts into air. It's a time when objects mean money, exchange value, pure circulation, and the wave of a plastic card over a scanner. Baudrillard calls our time period transparent because of the loss of the object to simulation, virtualization, satellitization, when "things" that have become virtual are spun into orbit, symbolized by the satellites themselves beaming our reality to us from "nowhere" as such. Paradoxically, as all that is solid melts into air, rather than being able to breathe easier, Baudrillard remarks on the obesity, saturation, and overabundance of a sick and stifled society:

> Protect everything, detect everything, contain everything—obsessional society.

> Save time. Save energy. Save money. Save our souls—phobic society.

> Low tar. Low energy. Low calories. Low sex. Low speed—anorexic society.[5]

We simulate the past, we simulate the future, and often the present moment is a simulation—mediated by technology, by inert acts of liking, friending, texting, surfing, blogging, gaming, viewing recorded performances. Everything needs advertising and all advertising is simulation. MTV is perfect because the advert and the product are the same thing—the doubling of simulation. Or else, while the reality is left behind, the business continues as usual, "as if," like the nightly news as the simulated form of what used to go by that name before total commercialization of the screened product and the need for infotainment—the loss of object, of real news, real politics, real sex, real trade, real presence. The transversality of loss occurs across all domains: economics, politics, sex—and with loss, inaction

5. Baudrillard, *America*, 41.

simulating action. Uploading and downloading, metaphors of lifting, where you do nothing except wait in front of a screen, maybe move a finger. The simulacrum (replacement of reality) stands in relation to simulation (what seems and is passed off as real), at a double remove from the real, as simulation and the simulacrum form their own closed circuit. Once upon a time, Marshall McLuhan said the medium is the message, but it is not clear any more what the message is or if there is meant to be one:

> Nobody is now the slightest bit interested in sexual liberation, political discussion, organic illnesses, or even conventional warfare (a fact for which we may be grateful so far as war in concerned: a good many wars will not have taken place merely because they held no interest for anyone). Our true phantasies lie elsewhere—specifically, they focus on the three above-mentioned forms [terrorism, transvestitism and cancer], each of which arises from the skewing of a basic operating principle and the confusion that results from this. These forms, terrorism, transvestitism, and cancer all reflect excesses—on the political, sexual and genetic levels respectively; they also reflect deficiencies in—and the consequent collapse of—the political, sexual and genetic realms.
>
> All these forms are viral—fascinating, indiscriminate—and their virulence is reinforced by their images, for the modern media have a viral force of their own, and their virulence is contagious.[6]

Talk about contagion . . . transversal contagion where the viral cuts across domains: the viral media, virtual objects "going viral"; and in the biological domain, AIDS, SARS,

6. Baudrillard, *Transparency of Evil*, 41.

Mad Cow; and across in the economy, the contagious fear that causes the market to melt down . . . talking of which, male meltdown into violence against women, into road rage, into rampage . . . in the technological domain nuclear meltdown, nondisposable toxic waste that takes ten thousand years to melt down and is lethal, while the meltdown of species and soils upon which humanity depends for life under man-made global warming hots up . . . "All these tendencies revolve around one generic scenario: catastrophe."[7]

And yet who cares? We all do, and our care is part of the turning of the wheel, picked up on, commodified, and sold back through the screen as information consumption, to enable us to care more and donate: money, sperm, reward points. But doing nothing, knowing someone somewhere is "doing something," is like doing something: simulation again.

Nothing is what it is; everything is engineered, designed, managed, manicured, airbrushed, curated, cut and pasted, speeded up for efficiency, and conversely out of date, disposable, so what we used to call forgotten is now merely detriment, discard, garbage for the bin man, whose gentrification under the name of United Resource Management (on the side of a Sydney garbage truck) is another simulation.

For soul work—the work of sensibility—the conditions are hard in the age of simulation and simulacra. For personal development, self-help fads become ways of coping, strategies (recalling that the word strategy is military) that we deploy (another military word) to stay on top, to look good, fit, young, ready—or just not to go under, simply to cope; but self-help and personal development and motivation seminars and practices are simulation as stimulation. We can end up addicted to them rather than empowered by them. The gym bod, the diet bod, the clothes, the hair, the makeover, and so on. It all has to be kept up, like keeping up

7. Ibid.

with everything else, the latest technology, the house prices, the endless apps for keeping up. It is no wonder so many people go crazy, crash out, get depressed, lose it, can't make it, feel lost, disoriented, forced to pretend, to put a face on it, to keep searching, to give up, to drop out, before they get shoved aside, or move to our own private Idaho or whatever.

Spirituality, by this token, is the luxury of the middle class, an indulgence like fine dining (another simulation), shopping therapy, or commodity fetishism, the Audi or the Lexus. On the other hand, we can see authentic spirituality is out there, we can see it on YouTube, we can walk the Camino or see the movie, or eat, love, pray, or see the movie; so even as we crash out or move state, we are tantalized by the spectacle of authenticity to be had. Maybe it would be better to live with Thich Nhat Hahn at Plum Village . . . maybe, but the simulacrum keeps us pulled in, and alternative lifestyles themselves all get commodified: Thich Nhat Hahn was whisked off to the world's best private hospital treatment in the United States after his stroke; but what about me? When Mother Teresa was about to die she was airlifted from Calcutta across to California and brought back to life. Not that they don't deserve it—they surely do—but even these authentic spiritual types are celebrities, like Hollywood A-listers, part of the simulacrum. Part of a world that, if we are outside it, we are alienated from it—even if the feeling is connectedness: another simulation. Alienation masked as connectedness keeps us on the outside without knowing it. While "connected" we feel "no one is watching," although the very things we are watching online leave us in no doubt it is a surveillance society; our (simulated) movements are all tracked. But this way of half being is part of the spectacle we spectate. Online is spectating. We become spectators of ourselves, curating our WeChat Moments or Instagram. We feel both part of something happening—our times—and apart from it: in touch and out of touch at the same time. And it is not like the real is elsewhere: it doesn't seem to be anywhere.

Ours is no longer the time for existential angst or existential authenticity. What then?

In the age of simulation and simulacra, the real is withdrawn. The imaginary—what we perceive as real, or think is real—has become hyper and dispersed. Perceptions and thoughts are partial and fragmented anyway, and in some sense, even distortions. We do not perceive the real or think it. But we do not realize that, which is why the simulacrum—the Matrix in the movie of it—can hold us in thrall. And if we have seen the movie (*The Matrix* or another) then we know it is an allegory of our simulacrum, our barcoding (*Dark Angel*), but this knowledge is just another mirror.

The symbolic, public reason, language as a shared symbolic order, the Protestant "public square" where reason among righteous folks can thrash out the right answer—when these become simulations, as they have become, they become mere sign, and the signs become capable of pointing everywhere and nowhere, disorienting, spacing us out while drawing us close, or seeming to. We are reduced to reading those little epigrams, those clever little comfort sayings, on Facebook or elsewhere, and trying to take heart; and meanwhile the real withdraws. Language and the symbolic are no locus of the real, either. Once they were, but not now.

This is where philosophy must have a therapeutic value. This is where philosophy interlocks with psychoanalysis, which grew out of it in the nineteenth century. But both have lost their savor. Psychoanalysis was severely devalued and eclipsed by American ego-psychology. Philosophy was sucked into the academy and suffered professionalization. Western religion—Christianity—too needs to retrieve its therapeutic value. Christianity became intellectually outsmarted by its own culture, the culture it gave rise to—of science and reason, secularity—and left behind, which is where it is today. Religious retrieval or revival would refer to the value of *mercy*, of going to the margins, of putting people before beliefs, and so on. Judaism talks about *tikkun Olam*, of mending the world. Christianity says faith, hope, and love are the basis for mending the world; both religions teach that this is not beyond us. But philosophy and religion by and large are stuck in a quandary, and what tends to rule instead is ideology on all sides, ideology being their politicization. And as the apostle Paul said, it is principalities and powers with which ultimately we struggle. Our demons today are ideologies we cannot see through and that possess us; writers from Dostoyevsky to Jung have emphasized this to great acclaim, so something is awakening.

It is not just that the planet is hotting up because of all the pollution and exploitation of nature by Big Capitalism: the *spiritual climate* is heating up as well. More and more people feel in their bones that something is afoot—the idea that we are in some kind of transition: either forward to something much better, like a New Age, or backward through some total catastrophe, to a new Dark Age—either way, something is afoot. This we call "awakening." Either we will destroy ourselves and go backward, or we will not and we will achieve some kind of new high tide mark in the sand (St. John Perse, *Amers*). We know, looking back, there are different ages, that the medieval world and the world of the Renaissance and the eighteenth-century Age of Reason were different ages and that one grew out of the other, out of the wreckage of the past, and the improvements on the past. We differentiate modern and postmodern, which is indicative of a slippage or shift in the tectonic plates of our being. So today millions of human beings around the world, billions perhaps, are connected and conscious of it in a way that is unprecedented in history. We chastise ourselves for polluting and wrecking the earth as much as we have, but we marvel at ourselves. There is a worldwide sense of potential, of possibility, of the future in our hands, of responsibility, of determination, of expectation.

Chapter 2

Signs of the Times

LACKING SOUL

O F THE THREE—PERSONALITY DEVELOPMENT, soul work, and spiritual practices—the one that often goes missing is soul work. Personality development and spiritual practices are socially recognized. *Personality development* happens at school in Western education and along with numeracy and literacy it is most important, although it is hardly mentioned as such by educationalists, because it is part of the schooling process, not a school subject. *Spiritual practices* are common, like meditation, yoga, in Catholicism keeping up with the daily liturgical cycle, in Judaism with the *parasha*, or pious practices like praying beads as in Catholicism, Buddhism, and Islam, or quasi-religious practices like surfing and other loner sports, or extreme sports in touch with nature, or endurance (to include jogging). But *soul work* is not so well recognized; it has been medicalized, reduced to counselling and psychotherapy. In other words, it is geared to the sick.

Positive psychology has developed as normal psychology, but the word "positive" gives it away as in thrall to positivism, behaviorism, and empirical metrics. As for the word "normal," what could be worse? From my point of view PP is not keyed to the soul but to consciousness, awareness, and the most popular of these positivisms, cognitive behavior therapy, says it all: that it has to do with the mind, cognition, knowledge, and ostensible self-knowledge, confused with self-consciousness, self-confidence, and self-esteem. It is all to do with self, not soul. The self is OK, but it is not soul. Soul cannot be OK. OK is not a soul word—let alone "I'm OK, You're OK."

The soul is keyed to wisdom, not knowledge; to dream and the dream center (Aryeh Kaplan), where it lives; to images (Hillman) and the letter in the unconscious (Lacan), not consciousness and propositions, but to unsayable truth (like that of theology), not correspondence truth (like that of phrenology); to the soul of the world, not the first person singular; to music—the music of the soul, which is tonal, melodic, harmonized; to sensibility, not the policing of behavior; to uncenteredness, not political correctness; to fantasy, not objectivity. In depth psychology or psychoanalytical terms positive psychology is mainly to do with strengthening the superego identifications. No coincidence, then, that positive psychology, cognitive behavior therapy, and the Pavlovian style of thinking that precedes them arise in the age of *the engineering of consent*, the age of the consumer, of advertising culture.[1]

Soul work has to do with the work of sensibility.[2] Soul sensibility is keyed to the arts—and in modern times, to developing or discovering our own creative potential. So it

1. Adam Curtis, "The Century of the Self," http://www.youtube.com/watch?v=eJ3RzGoQC4s&list=PLVY6n7Jrvk_RV_cvTfCW6vtnao1AztWpX.

2. The trap is aestheticism and "decadence," which European sensibility fell into at the end of the nineteenth century, especially in France, which led the way in this field.

is not simply a matter of developing the arts as "soul work" but of developing creativity. This has to do with that old philosophical chestnut, Knowing Thyself. To know myself means to know myself in my creativity, where my higher self shows itself. This is distinct from Western egoism, as in "finding yourself," and relates more closely to James Hillman's interpretation of Know Thyself to mean *find your eccentricity*. Finding your eccentricity is almost the opposite of superego identifications in positive psychology, tied to the symbolic order and what "they" might think and what "they" might say (Heidegger)—"they" (*das Man*) in scare quotes, as Heidegger famously explained in *Being and Time* (1927), are the superegoic characters (real and written) that hold our identity firm and together and allow us to believe in ourselves.

Finding your eccentricity is contrary to the spirituality of centering, and yet it is still egoic, perhaps even worse so, as the eccentric has to find his or her eccentricity at the expense of the normal and uneccentric and sensible. Finding your eccentricity is perhaps the luxury of those with rich parents, or of those who simply do not care (being closed in on themselves). The middle way between egocentricity and eccentricity is nonattachment or detachment, as every spiritual tradition teaches in unison—letting go the preoccupations of feelings and thoughts. Detachment (inner release of what holds me) is between my way and the highway. Inner release necessitates at the core of education a practice that will enable it. The point made in the previous chapter was that spiritual practices are better *after* or *along* with soul work, rather than *before* it or *instead* of it. Switching from being a developed personality—"full of personality"—to religious practices without the intervening and mediating soul work will not be conducive to well-being.

So we need to learn letting go (which is the essence of what Christians call forgiveness) but we need to let go soulfully, and that I think is what has been missing. A theology of forgiveness will not help us. A "task" of letting go will not enable us; no kind of pragmatic (again self-help) approach will work; it requires a wisdom practice. It is not enough for Eastern culture to come West: I have to journey East, not literally, but soulwise. I can do it soulwise without going there; yet I can go there but not do it soulwise. But how do I go East? I can live in the country of origin of the wisdom tradition dressed in some religious garb with a spiritual guru, but inwardly always remain the Presbyterian or Calvinist I was before I started, because I did the physical thing there, understood the intellectual part more or less, but never got the soul of it—or of myself—ever.

So there is this missing middle term: soul. And along with it, soul work, or soul-making. Soul is not something we have like an arm or a leg, but something we *need* like air, like friends, like health. Our life—our spirit—can be suffocated by a lack of soul as by a lack of air or too many comforts and "indispensable luxuries." We can be bereft or depressed by loss of soul as much as by no real friends, and soul can perish and wither like body organs. And yet, unlike air, friends, and body parts, the loss of soul can go unnoticed. Every outward loss everyone notices, while inward losses, of soul, are more subtle and escape notice, including our own.[3] This lack of sense of soul in religion, in psychology, in a utilitarian, functionalist, and efficiency-driven culture like ours means that soullessness is a sign of our times.

3. Kierkegaard, *Sickness Unto Death*, 62–3.

HEGEL

Figure 4. Friedrich Hegel with students.[4]

G. W. F. (Friedrich) Hegel is the philosopher of the signs of the times. Hegel's most famous work is the *Phenomenology of Spirit* (1807). All his other work—and a good deal of it is students' transcriptions of his lectures published posthumously—may be seen in some way or another as an expansion and explanation of this first major work. Hegel is one of the greatest thinkers of the Western canon. Plato and Aristotle, Kant and Hegel are the two great pairings. Different world philosophies issue from each and thence different worlds; but of course the pairings cross-fertilize each other and so these are the most generative thinkers. The order in which one might rank these four "Greats" would merely express one's philosophical predilections. These four form a *quadrivium*. Each is less without the other.

4. Lithographie F. Kugler. Das Wissen des 20. Jahrhunderts, Bildungslexikon, Rheda, 1931.

Hegel influenced Marx, whose ideas changed the map of the world in the twentieth century: the Russian revolutions and the Chinese revolutions and those elsewhere—Vietnam, Cuba, South America, Africa, and so on—were in his name, directly or indirectly. Marxism is not just Communism. Even more influential than Communism, Marx, under Hegel's sway, invented political journalism, which is now completely normative. Political journalism is the idea we all already hold that *news is not neutral*. If when you read the news and know it serves and legitimates certain interests, you are Marxian, even if you are a conservative. Today we would probably read certain news *because* it feeds our interests. Marxism is not just an ideology, as it has been with Communism: Marxism is a consciousness. It is political consciousness of power.

Marx and Marxian styles of critical thinking within sociology, such as those of the Frankfurt School (Adorno, Marcuse, Habermas), are deemed an interpretation of Hegel known as the Hegelian Left. On the Hegelian Right is the religious interpretation. One might legitimately hold that there could be no theosophy or New Age sensibility without Hegel's opening. Blavatsky's theosophy is a form of Hegelianism in the religious register. All the New Age philosophies of the nineteenth and twentieth centuries (theosophy, Steiner, Bailey, etc.) are Hegelian—on the Hegelian Right—because they all avail themselves of *master narratives*. Religions all have their own master narrative to begin with, particularly Christianity. Augustine's *City of God*, from the early fifth century, is the great text of the Christian master narrative, from "the beginning" (mythologized by the account in Genesis) to the "end of time" (mythologized by the account in Revelation). Christian culture's master narrative was taken up, then taken over, by the secular narrative of which there are competing and rival variants, visible in their political representation by and large, the main one today being that of the United Nations and its self-understanding and goals. Alice A. Bailey's New Age work written before the establishment of the United Nations paves the way for such a global governance or observation entity, as it intends also to pave the way for science and medicine to come. So there is a hidden affinity.

Hegel wrote the Master of master narratives that ostensibly took in other religions and their civilizations and cultures. People will argue with him on the detail, but that does not alter the perspective: Hegel opened a global-eyed view, a vista of the whole. What Hegel achieved was to conceive a Master Narrative that engulfed the Christian master narrative (which was "universal" after a Christian self-proclaimed fashion) and paved the way for a secular narrative that was at least more scientific and truly open and inclusive. The crux of Hegel is not that he purports to have a God's-eye view, or a prophetic vision, but that he takes it that *everything is linked with everything else*. Nothing exists "as such."

Kant just before Hegel, then Hegel following him, both rediscovered something of Eastern wisdom in their Western idiom. Kant rediscovered in Western philosophical idiom the Buddhist doctrine of *anatta* or nonself with his idea of the "unity of apperception," whereby the unity of our various numerous faculties constitute mind, and their unity is a form only, not a thing, not an "ego." The first person singular—"I" and "me"—are metaphors for this unity; they do not refer to something any more than the word "God" does (for God is not a thing [*res*], either). Hegel rediscovered what Thich Nhat Hanh the Zen master and peace activist calls "interbeing." This is the realization of Buddhism that everything is connected. Consider, for example, what went into my cup of green tea: the

manufacture of the cup in China from the earth; the painting, by hand, therefore the training that went into that; the
tradition of that training going back centuries maybe; or,
if factory-painted, then the funding, building, organization
and everything that needs to go on for a factory to exist
where my cup is painted by a machine; the machines themselves and where they come from; then there is the tea, into
which air, heat, earth, and water have contributed, and then
the picking, storing, packing, transporting. The person who
picked it, his or her mother, father, need for livelihood, so to
pick tea; the transportation: all that it takes to come by ship
or airplane. And that is just my cup of green tea. We can
ponder all things in terms of interbeing. Nothing just "is."
Hegel rediscovered this and called it Spirit (*Geist*). He also
realized that Spirit moves in time (all "things" that inter-are
are subject to time) and his account of the "phenomenology" (our sensuous apprehension) of Spirit is of something
always moving, changing, and directional.

SPIRIT

Hegel's view then we will call Spiritual (with a capital S,
just as *Geist* has a capital G in German, to remind us as we
read of the Hegelian inflection on the word), symbolizing
the interbeing of all living and dying. I should add that this
Spirit is nonrepresentational. What I mean is that Hegel is
like an abstract artist, Kadinsky or Mondrian, rather than a
representational artist. It is Hegel's philosophy that sets the
stage for abstract art, not the invention later of the camera,
as is often said. Without the camera, art would have gone
abstract because of Hegel's influence.[5] I refer here not to

5. I should add that Kant's influence on the invention of abstract
art is just as formative, because he dislocated beauty from the object
of representation and made a category of judgment in the play of

his philosophy of art, as such, but to his art of philosophy, his art of the concept. Hegel changes the notion of "abstraction." Before him, abstraction, as in medieval Scholasticism, was still representational, the words ostensibly representing definite ideas that could be held in mind. Not so Hegel: all Hegel's ideas are inseparable from one another. The ideas themselves are nonrepresentational. One has to stand before them, at the right distance (too close reading will not do) and let come to light what comes to light through the whole work. The difficulty is finding the right distance and the right angle, the difficulty of discernment. The problem with Hegel, as many readers of him display, is that you can read anything you like out of him including the idea that there is no such thing as an author (Foucault)—just like in abstract art, and the criticism of it, that if the artwork means everything and nothing, rather than something specifically represented, a child or a fool could have done as much.

Science is Hegelian too in that it relies on some kind of a guiding master narrative. So, for example, Darwin's evolution of species could not have been conceived without the preconceptions of Hegel in the background. Or astrophysics: very few people are interested in the math; but very many people are interested in the master narratives about the Big Bang, expanding universes, multiple dimensions, dark space, and so on, that astrophysics throws out. And all the permutations, refinements, and revisions of master narratives (all historiography therefore) continue the Hegelian presupposition about purposiveness. These presuppositions can be put in two words that are truly Hegelian in spirit: "development" and "progress." If we think how much a part of our vocabulary and even the very structure of our modes of expression these two words are, we have some

---

the faculties. This opened the door to a revolution in art. Hegel then jammed the door open.

gauge of Hegel's influence. Hegel is not in the past; he is *in us* insofar as we speak.

Even the reactions to Hegel, starting in his own lifetime with Kierkegaard, then Schopenhauer, and later analytical philosophy, more or less presuppose him as *their negative*.

And the power of the negative—the listlessness and *errancy* of the negative—was precisely part of Hegel's own philosophy. The negative or unconscious or forgotten aspect of a phenomenon—especially of Spirit—Hegel said is *generative*; the negative plays into the mix of what happens and what eventuates. Nothing is not simply nothing: it plays ultimately the more powerful part in we say now "deconstructing" (Derrida) stabilities, certainties, self-evidences, positivities, so that none of these in Hegel's sense are *true*. The true lies before us in time. Its traces lie behind and all around. We more or less recognize them. But every act is a seed, it is generative of other's thoughts and consequent actions or inactions. Hegel rediscovers the Eastern sense of karma. Karma is not a philosophy of "cause and effect"— that is Western logical rationalism. Karma is the philosophy of interactivity predicated on the understanding of interbeing. Understanding interbeing leads to the importance of inaction that the East has always known and that totally draws a blank with the American "can do" mentality today.

The idea of the *Zeitgeist*—the Spirit of the times—is Hegelian. In the context of Hegel's philosophy this idea has an aspect we might not be aware of. The essence of Hegel's philosophy is that there exists a Spirit—call it life, call it mind, call it what you will—that is not all-encompassing, which does not incorporate all living beings and all active intellects, but weaves *in, through, and among* all that is and that is not "natural" in some set way that accords with the eponymous "laws of nature," but is spiritual, that is moving, living, outworking itself through us, through the world, through all beings, we might say. But the truth for Hegel is in the weave that leaves nothing out and *the weave is where the real* is—not here or there.

This is different from the idea of cosmos, which is the idea of the unity of all being, the great chain of being from earth to the heavens; Hegel's idea is generative, it is moving, it is becoming. This oneness is not now, it is not yet. The Spirit is working toward it through the "means" of life. It is in this context that he speaks of *the signs of the times*. The signs of the times are not read *qua* ourselves so much as the outworking of the World Spirit, or Absolute Spirit. Hegel uses different key words for what he has in mind in order to bring it into view for his reader; his language is not merely a terminology, any more than his philosophy is a system in the post-Hegelian sense of "systematic theology" or "systems theory."

So everything is connected, but not cosmically, not as an order of being, but dynamically, in terms of change and externalization: from past to future, from within to without. Hegel puts creation before cosmos, becoming before being.

TIME

This is where time comes in—timing, timeliness, time-boundedness. Hegel is a philosopher of time—or more precisely, a philosopher of history, as we, being human, can only really conceive of time as the eternal return of the same or as history. Since the advent of Judaism, history has taken over the world, for better or worse: the jury is still out on that one. Nietzsche thought Christianity had failed Christ's mission to save the world from sin, and Heidegger expanded this to the idea that Christianity had now (from the twentieth century) made the world impossible to save—our hungry wartorn world chock-full of bombs and war machines, nuclear power stations and devastated lands and oceans. Signs of the times: the reign of disfigurement, illusion, good old-fashioned evil.

We can't see time; it is a condition of our seeing (Kant). But we can see history. What we call history is where Spirit is outworking, and the signs of the times are the signs of this outworking of Spirit. The whole notion of the externalization of Spirit in history speaks of *event*. Christianity is the superior religion for Hegel because it is founded on events. "Christ" is the name of events concerning Jesus, who, in that sense, metaphorically speaking, is an "incarnation" of the meaning of those events, the meaning of which gives rise to the discourse of theology, which the apostle Paul inaugurates almost immediately so that his writings (and that of other New Testament authors) can be seen as themselves foundational, and the New Testament itself as foundational, the mistake of Protestantism, which turns Christianity into a book religion. The event does not represent the Spirit but enacts it, and only with hindsight, Hegel avers, are we wise: his famous Owl of Minerva in *The Philosophy of Right* spreads its wings only with the falling of dusk.

We see time in its irreversibility. Negatively, not seeing time puts it into the same bracket as Christian *pistis* (faith), which also operates on the basis of *not-knowing*. Faith is *a*gnostic: the middle way between knowledge and total ignorance. Similarly, Hegel's philosophy is pitched less to knowledge than *recognition*, and in this he is Platonic. When we *recognize* we do not yet know, nor are we any longer unaware. The "not yet" and "any longer" indicate time. The time factor is always involved in Hegel's thinking. We recognize something because this human (rather than Christian) "faith" has us "working in the dark." Just like in a dark room we recognize objects, so with the signs of the times. The signs of the times always have to do with the

Spirit, which, if we want to say we know it—and our grammar forces us to this pitch—then we know it in "the weave," not in any way *as such*: in the weave of interconnections, interconnectedness, interbeing.

Knowledge is cognitive and establishes or believe in "facts," and facts are separable and separate items, but recognition is soulful. Recognition recognizes not "the facts" but the shape of things, the way of things, the weave. Again, Hegel picks something from the East: his notion of recognition means the light switching on, enlightenment, realization. To repeat, this is not enlightenment as knowledge, but a realization, a new light of mind that casts a shadow and perspective on "the known" and "unknown." It knows them in inverted commas, by way of recognition, in their outlines or de-lineaments only, the way we recognize a face from its silhouette.

On the human level there is a unity, but in time, between people, a unity of empathy, which is the reverse imprint of love, which is active and personal. Evil is what undoes empathy, while empathy is what makes us adult. Our empathy with one another is the basis of mending the world (*tikkun Olam*) or the movement of the Spirit, which "wants" the good, but is contingent in that sense on "what happens," which may be for the worse, like nuclear power for example, or the eradication of species for short-term monetary gain. The opposite of the Spirit is illusion and glamour—again, a sense from the East that comes West with Hegelian thinking.

BACK TO SOUL

If we now return to what I was saying at the outset about soul work and spiritual practices, and consider it against this background, we would need to conclude that our spiritual practices need to be keyed to the time. They do not operate in static space or cosmos. If we think they do, we fool ourselves. Our spiritual practices either take us and history *forward*— for we *are* the history-makers, each and every one of us, *in* each and *by* each and every one of our daily actions—*or* our spiritual practices pull us back. If we do spiritual practices in a regressive space-time, it will involve a certain unconsciousness that is not itself spiritual—although, for Hegel, even that which is a drag on the Spirit and is regressive is in the mix, and does not hinder the eventual outworking, as the outworking is not given in advance, but given *qua* our human endeavors. And if nothing else, what we perceive as our suffering will teach us. Each time it seems "history repeats itself" the screw turns, the suffering becomes more acute.

In Hegelian terms, soul work must beware of being merely a form of nostalgia. That is its big temptation. The soul in soul work must be *buoyant*. The soul should *buoy up* the Spirit. The soul is not subservient to the Spirit then; remembering the Spirit is not a predetermination for Hegel. I would add that the soul and soul work are constitutive for how Spirit works itself out. Soul work needs therefore to be *keyed* to the Spirit—that is to say *attuned*. Nevertheless, it is important to realize that attunement to the Spirit is not what is generally meant when one talks about "my spirituality." I think this is where Hegel is important to understanding the harmonization of personality, soul, and spirit and rethinking spirit—which Christian theology has made synonymous with a "ghost" as in Holy Ghost—with a non-representational concept of Spirit.

For Hegel there is a god, but whether it is the God of Christianity or not is hard to say. In any case God is not behind us like an origin, like a ready-made, like a deity; God for Hegel is ahead, yet to be known. Religions may have some revelation of God, but this revelation is part of the road, part of the journey to the God, who lies ahead of us. Speaking of the Christian version of God, André Gide wrote in his famous *Journal* for 1916, "God is not behind us. He is to come [. . .] He is terminal and not initial. He is the supreme and final point toward which all nature tends in time [. . .] It is through man that God is moulded" (Sunday, January 30). Also speaking of the Christian culture and the Christian version of God, the great poet Rainer Maria Rilke wrote in 1910 in *The Notebook of Malte Laurids Brigge*, "Is it possible that we say 'women', 'children', 'boys', not guessing (despite all our culture, not guessing) that these words have long since had no plural, but only countless singulars? Yes it is possible. Is it possible that there are people who speak of 'God' and mean something they have in common? [. . .] Yes it is possible."[6] This "Yes it is possible" is a heavy sigh!— for a world in which God had become idea, and religious, a God-believing world about to embark on mass murder on a heightened and historic scale.

Rabbi Jonathan Sacks reiterates Gide and Rilke in his own way. The definition of God (of all that is good and to be hoped for) is not some "deposit of revelation" (the ugly term used by some Christians) whereby the present and future are forever pulled back in a regressive and prideful stance that believes it has custody of the truth on behalf of everyone else. This is the death of God (Nietzsche). When Moses meets God in the Burning Bush at the origin of the Judeo-Christian tradition, and asks who God is:

> God's reply, *Ehyeh asher ehyeh*, is often trans-
> lated as 'I am who I am'. This entirely misses the
> point of the original which literally means 'I will
> be what I will be'. God exists in the future tense,
> because he is a God of freedom. God is not part
> of nature. He created nature. Therefore he stands

6. Rilke, *Notebook of Malte Laurids Brigge*, 23.

> outside it. He is not bound by it. He is free. And
> to the extent that we are in God's image, we too
> are free. The gift God gives us is freedom itself.
> We too will be what we choose to be.[7]

The strength of Hegel's philosophy—why it remains two hundred years later (itself a sign of the times)—is that he totally *gets* this. Obversely, this is why old-fashioned Christianity religiously avoids reading Hegel in ministerial training schools—if it does not avoid philosophy altogether!

Modern Christianity shows the very opposite of soulful buoyancy with its static "past tense" view of God and revelation as a protected "deposit"—what philosophers critically call its ontotheology. And the fact that no churches admit this or ask why it has been this way or has to be this way, but carry on much as usual, is a problem of religion, of our own religion, the religion of the language I write in, English, *as a sign of our time.*

Hegel avoided the religious fallacy that says there is no truth higher than religion. Anachronistically speaking (for he preceded it), Hegel also avoided the theosophical fallacy that holds there is no religion higher than truth. The former has its hands full of itself, the latter is left empty-handed. Hegel had a Gemini wisdom for he had one hand half full and the other half empty, and the two working in exchange. These cross purposes according to which the world works are called Hegelian dialectic.

The revelations of religion are not terminus points, or else religious revelations would mark the end of history, which they do not. The revelations of religion are way marks, pointers on the way, but the way is greater than any one way. Christianity was originally called The Way, according to the author Luke in the New Testament. The three Abrahamic religions have ultimate and final revelations,

7. Sacks, *Home We Build Together*, 58.

and from Hegel's point of view these are ultimate and final for the believers, but not for God, not for the earth; not either therefore for Hegel's Absolute Spirit, the final term of the nonrepresentation that we have in mind.

Hegel did rank religions though. He did not believe religions were all equal or each relative perspectives on the same thing. He ranked religions according to the extent to which they were keyed to his Absolute Spirit, the extent to which religions were spiritually generative. If religions were not spiritual in his sense, then they were regressive and on the wrong side of history, because history is going somewhere, like it or not. In this sense Hegel's philosophy is a critique of religion, because it provides a measure of them. Hegel might have developed his thought further in this area had he lived longer.

If we take Hegel's philosophy as woven into the linguistic and perceptual givens of modern consciousness, then how does soul tie in with it and harmonize? Well there is no recipe or final answer in line with the question.

But the soul wants something *more* than solidarity. The soul wants to be consecrated. Consecration is what the Holy Spirit does to the soul in Christianity and what by Hegel we *recognize* in history as the Great Soul, the genius. The Great Soul may not be Napoleon, as Hegel's detractors mock, given he used that example. It may be Schubert. It may be the forgotten soul. It may be the Jewish tradition of the *lamed vavnik*: the twenty-two righteous men, usually beggars, but for whose virtue God would destroy the world in pain at its sin. Genius may be forgotten or hidden—like the soul then. The point is that consecration *for* the soul, however we get it, is an *initiation*. Initiation, known to all religions, refers to the *soul's contact with the real*. This is what Hegel's nonrepresentational Spirit points toward: the spirit in the real that sets us—one soul at a time—apart from the "way of the world," and attunes us to the signs of the times and thereby orients us in action and livelihood. For Christians, this is the Holy Spirit of Christian enthusiasm; for Buddhists, it is mindfulness energy. Whatever the word for what is nonrepresentational here, which Hegel called Spirit, the fact is that consecration of the soul is bestowed, and this *happens* as a benediction; it may not be won or earned or achieved. But, as Plato pointed out at the start of philosophy, it can be faked.

Chapter 3

Bel Canto

The song is where the soul is today.

PRELUDE

OUR FAVORITE SONGS ARE matters of taste.
Our taste is a matter of sensibility.
Sensibility is partly inherited, partly learned, partly earned.

It has to do with what we enjoy and what we love,

Which has to do with our destiny.

Destiny counters biology.

Our biology has to do with our ancestry,

With where we were physically from, from way back,

The conditions of life over centuries to which our ancestors had to adapt.

Our biology is our heritage that draws us back by the body.

Our destiny draws us forward by the soul.

Taste stands between, in the moment we know now and enjoy.

Good taste harmonizes, it can ease our soul.

There is a song by The Grateful Dead, "So Many Roads" that is about the roads we take in life, the many roads that ease our soul.

Taste is not just a matter of taste: it is a matter of world, our world, the world, the world gone by, and the world to come. The song that appeals to our good taste soothes, softens, celebrates, brings back memories, recalls to mind, relives. But also a song is a foretaste of time to come, of unknown roads ahead.

Later I refer to specific songs. The point is not to enforce my taste. My choices were in any case governed by other considerations than taste: principally, to indirectly connect song to soul, and vice versa. The point of that is to illustrate song is where the soul is. To connect song to soul is to connect song to soul work and soul-making.

The great American poet and activist Gary Snyder said the true thinkers, poets, and artists are not on the left or the right: they are *ahead*. And he is a prime example.

Everything is breathing. We can hear it if we listen deeply to the earth. This kind of listening takes training. Such training is called meditation. Breath carries the song. Singing is something humans have in common with birds. The song allows us to fly, to soar skyward, to fly like an eagle, or like a swallow, dipping and diving, or like a robin redbreast, prettily fluttering; but song is the way of our transcendence in the old religious metaphysical language, or as the poet Mallarmé put it, our *azure*.

RECAPITULATION

Soul-making, as I have been saying, is the work we need to do before we talk about spirituality. In our time—of growing soullessness—"the desert grows," as the German poet Hölderlin said. In the spirit of Hölderlin, the modern philosopher

Martin Heidegger devoted whole lecture courses to this sense of the nihilism at the heart of modernity and modern technical functionalist culture, for which art he thought had some "saving power." I think so of song. So whether you are in the clutches of the growing wasteland or into New Age spirituality or happily ensconced in conventional religion, or whether none of this has ever occurred to you (so that you therefore collude with the wasteland), in my philosophy as therapy the song is where the soul is and there is no spirituality (and no authentic Western religiosity) without soul.

What is soul? Soul is the unison of our sensibilities and inner sensitivity. Taste is linked to this. So-called bad taste is linked to a total lack of inner sensitivity. Soul is the unison of sensibilities, not the unity, because we are not unified, but enigmas to ourselves. We only really know ourselves through our sensibility—if then.

Spirituality has become self-help. The self is a control factor, a social construction largely, a mask. Soul is not self, nor is soul a thing we have; rather soul is what we are. Soulful is reflective (like the moon), and has to do with passion/passivity (which are related), hiddenness, modesty, occlusion. Soul is a nexus of inner attunements.

ABSOLUTE MUSIC

Music went ahead of song in the nineteenth century.

Music came of age in the West with *absolute music*, the most famous name attached to which is Beethoven. Absolute music is music that is not *for* something, such as occasional music, or church music, or court music, and is not *about* anything (which is called program music). Absolute music is music set free from outer constraints to sound the inner being of the world on its own terms—that of *melody*. Unchained melody.

"Harmonic melody," Richard Wagner called it: "melody detached from spoken verse . . . of infinite expression and infinite treatment."[1] The nineteenth-century philosopher Schopenhauer, the first to write philosophically of music and the also the first philosopher of sex, speaks of two universalities. The first is a universality of concepts and the second a universality of music. *Logos* and *melos*.

Absolute music is *melos* set free. *Melos* set free from *logos*, from words. Wagner: "As long as the word held sway [under Christianity] its rule was alpha and omega; when it sank into the bottomless depths of harmony, when it became no more than the moaning and sighing of the soul— at the most fiery heights of Catholic church music—the word was wilfully hoisted atop those harmonic columns and slung from wave to wave of rhythmless melody."[2] Note: we are talking about *rhythmless melody* now.

What prefigured absolute music more than anything were the Burgundian choristers in the fifteenth century. They developed skills in counterpoint with voices, treating the voices like instruments, so that in fact the words became music or perfectly "transparent" to the music.

This was a problem for the Catholic Church, as the liturgy became *too musical* in a sense: you could not hear the words properly, and so at the reforming Council of Trent in the mid-sixteenth-century words were reasserted over music—*logos* over *melos*. The exemplar of the reassertion of *logos* over *melos* was Palestrina. In his sublime music, *logos* is nevertheless reinstated over *melos*. While Palestrina is the name associated with the heights of Catholic Church music, actually it was its death knell. After Palestrina *melos* as a force in its own right shifted out of the church. Just as science had shifted out of Christianity after the Galileo

1. Wagner, *Artwork of the Future*, 40.
2. Ibid., 36.

inquisition, and entered into the secular sphere, music after its shift to the secular sphere found new freedom through works of Rameau, Haydn, Mozart, and others. Prior to them, J. S. Bach, from within the Protestant Church had paved the way for musical development. Bach did technically about everything it was possible to do in musical form and changed all the forms he touched at the same time.

Beethoven, taking over the new sonata form from Haydn and Mozart, succeeded in endowing it with more dramatic substance that involved the listener than ever heard before, going beyond the powers of dramatic vocal music. *This is where song got left behind and the development of music outstripped song* through "the immeasurable capacity of instrumental music to express elemental forces and passions" (Wagner).[3] Absolute music transported the listener to a realm outside him-or herself. The songs of the day (lieder) could not compete.

Lieder are usually understood as exemplifying the romantic art song—songs of love, of longing, and of the beauty of nature and woman. They were the popular music of the day. But to our ears—unless we are "specialists" trained to know better (and then we will be on the defensive)—lieder sound like the German, or French, or English songs of another world before the world wars and modernity proper.

3. Ibid., 40. What characterizes Wagner's melody is its potentially "eternal" (German: *unendliche*) duration, i.e., any stop is more or less arbitrary. It is based on his unprecedented facility with wandering seamlessly through different tonalities without halting for a key change.

**Figure 5. Ian Bostridge singing "Erlkönig,"
a poem by Goethe from 1782, set to music by Schubert.**[4]

The poem that Bostridge sings is somewhat Gothic, therefore uncharacteristic of its author, Goethe. A father and son ride home by dark on horseback, the son is afflicted, the father urgent, though by what and why is uncertain, and the son dies in his arms as they ride. Goethe, Schubert, Bostridge. This is the genre that is lieder at its best. The strident opening piano chords could almost foreshadow Little Richard, were not the shadow rather stretched by the comparison. Occasionally in nineteenth-century music (though less in song) we can hear, or think we can hear, a presentiment of the impossible: jazz. Whether this is the case or not, the point I want to go on and make is that there is a discontinuity between lieder and the modern song.

In the nineteenth century Schopenhauer wrote influentially on music, influencing Wagner, who, in turn,

4. https://www.youtube.com/watch?v=mmx4MN3xZpM.

influenced all the arts and beyond. Schopenhauer thought that *music manifested the inner being of the world* and with it our inner oneness with the world and with one another, and that future post-Christendom civilization in the West and right around the world—what today we would signify as global culture—would be founded on *melos*. Music unites; ideas (words) divide. "Music," Schopenhauer wrote, "gives the innermost kernel preceding all form, or the heart of things."[5] Music *gives* before and beyond reason.

So to sum up, while *melos* was set free from *logos* in nineteenth-century art music, the song lagged behind, not having developed significantly since the troubadours—apart from opera that is, where the sound of the voice and the new operatic singing were invested with huge emotional energy. Wagner was aware of this, but Italian was the great operatic language. The emotional energy of opera was hampered by its "stageyness" (technological lack) and musically reached occasional heights: the great arias. Otherwise the music was a quite mundane accompaniment on the whole. This is the situation Wagner tried to break out of by raising opera to the heights of the music drama, to a higher order of synthesis of arts, and he succeeded or not, depending on your taste.

THE AMERICAN CENTURY

Two contributions from the Old World fed into the Jazz Age, the new age of music, the American Age. First was *impressionistic harmony* in composers like Ravel and Debussy and Satie, primarily the French school, after Wagner. Debussy's *Clair de lune* would be a prime example. Impressionistic harmony (remembering impressionism in painting associated with Manet and Monet was also appearing around this

5. Schopenhauer, *World as Will and Representation*, 1:263.

time) was already a break with the formal structures of art music, just as impressionistic painting had to go outside the official Paris Salon and found the *Salon des refusés* (Salon of the rejected). What jazz then did was *marry impressionistic harmonies with rhythm*, but jazz is inconceivable without first the development out of Wagner down from absolute music of impressionistic harmonies.

The pianists had a big play in this regard. The great pianists of the nineteenth century, of whom the greatest, Liszt, was Wagner's brother-in-law, and the greatest piano pieces, like Beethoven's piano sonatas or Chopin's nocturnes, point toward the next stage of music, which was not as it turned out the new formalism of the modernists, their academicization, intellectualization, and professionalization of music, but the new popularity of the song, *and jazzing of the music*, on the piano: Oscar Peterson, the blind Art Tatum, the slightly deranged Thelonius Monk, Bill Evans in a world of his own, a bit like Glen Gould playing Bach on the piano. They jazzed the old standards on the piano. Many great jazz performers cross genres; perhaps best known in this regard is Keith Jarrett.

The second contribution of the Old World to the Jazz Age was with the exploitation of the gap between the written score and its execution. *Rubato* is an Italian word associated with Chopin's scoring. Its meaning is obscure. It is about the tension underneath and playing out of that, rather than strictly playing the notes on the page. Technically *rubato* allows the classical musician leeway to produce tension by starting in a split second early or late. The greatest singers are not the best and most perfect, but those with slight release from the rules; Sinatra's timing and phrasing is a standout example.

And one more point: in the Jazz Age, just like in the nineteenth century, the songwriters and performers and musicians of the era of the American Songbook were naturals. Often too they had genius. Louis Armstrong, whose performing career spanned fifty years, is thought to have influenced the entirety of jazz and song in some way. Armstrong dropped out of school at eleven and started singing in the street. This is like the nineteenth century. Wagner had some early training but mainly taught himself music and conducting. He wrote a piano transcription of Beethoven's massive Ninth Symphony when he was still in his teens. These composer-musicians did not come from the elites, but from ordinary backgrounds or obscurity. Wagner was not sure who his father was. Louis Armstrong was the son of a New Orleans prostitute. Jimi Hendrix learnt to play the guitar upside-down because no one showed him how to hold it, yet he became the instrument's supreme exponent.

THE GREAT AMERICAN SONGBOOK

Despite the precursory contributions I have just noted, the modern popular song is not continuous with the century before it. The modern popular song goes back behind the classic and church-derived tradition of singing in choir and picks up from the troubadour tradition of the minstrel and marketplace and comes out of that more than it does lieder. Music here *accompanied* the song. Song developed in the seventeenth century (Monteverdi) into the opera aria. Verdi composed enchanting and soulful melodies in his arias that required fairly minimal orchestral backup to provide a bit of rhythmic enhancement. For this reason the music in his various operas sounds similar and recognizable from opera to opera; what is different are the melodies of the great arias that stand out from the operas in which they belong. Shortly we shall see how this feature was reiterated in the age of the Great American Songbook with regard to songs in movies.

Whatever the influences on the Great American Songbook, the fact is this: *The song in the sense we experience it today and largely take for granted is a relatively new phenomenon.*

What and *when* was the "Great American Songbook"? Let us clarify these questions. The term "Great American Songbook" refers generically to the most important and influential American popular songs, the so-called standards, in any popular genre indicated by sales charts, from the 1920s to the 1950s and the advent of rock 'n' roll. However, as we shall see here, the Great American Songbook extends much later than the 1950s, into the 1970s and 1980s, as the standards were rerecorded and new standards produced and set. As new and unprecedented as it was unexpected, *the opening of the Great American Songbook is the great musical event of the twentieth century*. As such, I claim it is one of the great soul-making events too. It is what gives us to say *the song is where the soul is*.

Behind the opening of the Great American Songbook, in the usual account of it, there is a confluence of influences: the great African-American hymns and old Negro spirituals, Cajun, country, blues, folk, and from the cities, where it was all happening, showtime, and later, the movies, and most important of all, jazz. Jazz was not so much a noun then as a verb. Something you did to music to loosen it and free it up.

What happened was that in America *melos* and *rhythmos* joined forces before *logos* joined them. First *melos* and *rhythmos* joined forces in New Orleans jazz, dance, and ragtime. But then the voice was added: the jazz singer—Louis Armstrong, Billie Holiday. In the 1930s and 1940s, the heyday of the Jazz era, The Ink Spots were jazz too, but harked back to pre-classical forms with their unaccompanied voices, in what was then called "barbershop," with its *a capella* ("in chapel style") harmonious singing. Traditionally instruments accompanied the chorus; The Ink Spots at least had a double bass to keep a four-beat-to-the-bar rhythm.

The unity of these three, *melos, rhythmos,* and *logos,* was the ideal, going back to ancient Greek culture. It is worth remembering that Greek poetry was sung—the sad fact of only the text surviving deprives us of genuine insight into the holy trinity of *melos, rhythmos,* and *logos.*

With the opening of the Great American Songbook, the unification of *melos* and *rhythmos* with *logos* came into play in unprecedented kinds of song with *deeply emotive* accompanying melody, which here perhaps harked back to Verdi at his best—as far as expressiveness goes. This expressiveness and emotional expressivity would have been different from the Greeks, for whom *melos, rhythmos,* and *logos* would have had ritualistic meaning.

In the Great American Songbook *expressiveness became all important.* It was the personality of the song that counted now, just as the personality of the singer became crucial, hence the star and celebrity system that emerged. Lieder, by contrast, have the quality of impersonality: they are recited. You go to a *recital* of lieder rather than to a performance; lieder are sung from the heart in a different sort of way from the American popular song, which is supposed to be individual and personal. It expresses.

Let us take for example Nat King Cole—one of the greatest singers we can have ever heard. And note how absolutely and utterly different he is from the lieder we have just heard. Nat evinces a whole other world.

Figure 6. Nat King Cole singing "Unforgettable."[6]

When Nat sings the first word "unforgettable," it is unforgettable. It is impossible to imitate, because it is stamped all over with his personality. No one else sounds like this, and if they do, they become pale imitators. Nat King Cole owns the song. He owns songs like "When I Fall in Love,"[7] or "The Very Thought of You," because sung by him these songs are unforgettable! He owns them in the sense that he captures their beauty and so we love his renditions above all. There is not some "standard of perfection" here. It's a uniqueness that transmits soul to soul. The popularity of Nat King Cole's classics is not a marketing strategy at all (there was not one to speak of): it is a tribute to the many hearts his voice captured and keeps capturing. This is a soul phenomenon. His voice wins hearts and every heart won

6. https://www.youtube.com/watch?v=Fy_JRGjc1To.

7. https://www.youtube.com/watch?v=GfAbogNPy6s.

feels better, revived, loving and loved, when it hears the songs.

The popular song is the result of the union of *melos*, *rhythmos*, and *logos* with deeply emotive voice and melody. *This is the primary feature of the songs of the Great American Songbook.* And it is discontinuous in relation to the past. It is a new event. And the songs belong to a new culture of freedom in America. Fred Astaire and Ginger Rogers or Rita Hayworth danced to the new songs and new music in new American styles that took the world by storm and remain the very meaning of modern dance worldwide.[8] This is the true meaning of "modern" as well, the popular meaning, not the pretentious meaning Adorno and the modernist critics of so-called "serious music" in Old Europe tried to give it by the intellectualist turn they foisted on classical music in Europe. In songs like those by Nat King Cole, *song reached its truth.* This is where we find soul and soulfulness today—just as folks did back in his day.

America is often ridiculed in Europe for a lack of culture, for the Disneyfication of the world, for kitsch and sentiment, for having to buy culture and import it, but the Great American Songbook is a cultural achievement as great as anything achieved anywhere else by any other civilization, and actually a lot more important than many American inventions. The Great American Songbook is a supreme cultural achievement by any standards.

Into this confluence of musical influences in America and new social freedom to invent, change, and innovate stepped the great songwriters: Irving Berlin, Hoagy Carmichael, the Gershwins, Jerome Kern, Johnny Mercer, Cole Porter, Rodgers and Hart, Rodgers and Hammerstein, and so on. Then there were the singers: Bing, Nat, Billy (Lady Day),

8. For Fred Astaire and Rita Hayworth dancing the bossa nova, see https://www.youtube.com/watch?v=ILbvtB_opKk.

Ella, Frank Sinatra, Sammy Davis Jr. (Mr. Bojangles), Al Jol-
son, Peggy Lee, Ivie Anderson, Ethel Waters—a list that goes
on and on and leads into the rock era: the singer-songwriters,
Chuck Berry, later Bob Dylan, and so on. Duke Ellington
deserves a special mention—perhaps the twentieth century's
supreme impresario, bandleader, and composer.

A word about the rendition and the cover. The truth
of the modern song is in the rendition (which may be a live
performance or a recording). The singer captures the song
in a way that is popular because everyone can hear and recognize it. How and why they do is a mystery that explanation falls short of. The standout example is Sinatra's "My
Way," a Paul Anka song. Robbie Williams sang it—among
the few who would take the risk—but it remains Sinatra's
song.

Covers are interesting in this regard. Whose cover is
best? "Stardust" by Hoagy Carmichael is the most covered
song in the Great American Songbook. Personally I like
Hoagy's rendition better than any cover I have heard—and
it has been covered by the greatest singers. "Send in the
Clowns" is a difficult song to sing, written by Stephen Sond-
heim for the 1973 Broadway musical, *A Little Night Music*.
The song uses complex compound meters and switches
between them, and the singer has to somehow communi-
cate the disillusionment, bitterness, and regret of her life.
The song has been covered by the greats, by Bing Crosby,
Frank Sinatra (who got a gold record with it in 1974),
Shirley Bassey, Sarah Vaughan, Judy Collins, Liz Taylor,
Grace Jones, Tom Jones, Olivia Newton-John, and others.
But Barbara ("Barbra") Streisand's cover shows why many
regard her as the twentieth century's greatest female popular singer. For her concert performances Sondheim wrote
an extra verse, and there is a studio recording by her on
her 1986 album, *The Broadway Album*. Streisand suffered

stage fright late in her career that incapacitated her, so she performed more and more rarely; the added verse speaks to this. It's her song.

If you can find this footage on YouTube or elsewhere from 1986, where she sings straight into the camera, then you will find it is a stunning performance by the highest standards of the song and singing. Watch her eyes.

Figure 7. Barbra Streisand singing "Send in the Clowns."[9]

THE KOREAN SCENE

Since the opening of the Great American Songbook the song in the American sense has blossomed all around the world in every country.

In South Korea, to take perhaps the primary example, young Korean singers have taken over the pop song with

9. https://www.youtube.com/watch?v=UBkMokuIAY8.

renewed vigor and creativity, and I think they have set a
new standard for the ballad, in both the male and female
registers as well as in duets.

On February 22, 2005, the Korean actress and celebrity Lee Eun-ju committed suicide, aged twenty-four, just
a few days after her graduation from university. She left a
suicide note scrawled in blood, in which she wrote, "Mom,
I am sorry and I love you."[10] To quote a blog: "The news
of her death prompted a massive outpouring of grief from
fellow actors, film makers and fans. Hundreds of fellow actors and entertainers attended Lee Eun-ju's funeral where
vocalist Bada sang the song [. . .] 'You Were Born to be
Loved' and friends spoke in her memory. Her friends and
colleagues have held memorials for her every year ever
since her death."[11]

Below, Lee Eun-Ju is pictured; the video was put together by a fan, Samsonchanys, with Bada singing.

10. https://en.wikipedia.org/wiki/Lee_Eun-ju.

11. Blog by Doejo Barr in comments at https://www.youtube.com/
watch?v=A5FH8–10Jvk retrieved 12/Feb/2016.

Figure 8. Bada singing "You Were Born to Be Loved."[12]

Here are the lyrics in Korean, English, Japanese, and Chinese:

❀ঌ 당신은 사랑받기 위해 태어난 사람
(You were born to be loved)

당신은 사랑 받기 위해 태어난 사람
You were born to be loved
きみは愛されるため生まれた
你是为爱而生

당신의 삶속에서 그사랑받고 있지요
Within your life, you've been receiving His love
きみの生涯は愛で満ちている
在你的生命中, 你已接受他的爱

태초부터 시작된 하나님의 사랑은
The love of God has began [sic] since creation
永遠の神の愛は
在万物被创造的那一刻起上帝的爱就已存在

12. https://www.youtube.com/watch?v=A5FH8-10Jvk.

우리의 만남을 통해 열매를 맺고
And has connected with us through our fellowship
われらの出会いの中で実を結ぶ
随著我们友谊的成熟

당신이 이 세상에 존재함으로 인해
Because of your existence in this world
きみの存在が
因为你在地球上的存在

우리에겐 얼마나 큰 기쁨이 되는지
We share this great joy among us
私にはどれほど大きな喜びでしょう
我们共度了快乐的时光

당신은 사랑받기 위해 태어난 사람
You were born to be loved
きみは愛されるため生まれた
你是因为上帝的爱而诞生[13]

The lead singer of SNSD (So Nyuh Shi Dae, 소녀시대), the Korean pop group of nine girls known as "Girls Generation," is on the panel of the variety show, "Star King." She says she can sing the song "You Were Born to Be Loved" and everyone wants to hear her do so. The MC passes her the microphone and she sings the first verse. This was possibly the most riveting twenty-three seconds in the entire two hundred episodes of the show to date—certainly for her fans.[14] *Suddenly it is Taeyeon's song.*

---

13. Lyrics from http://kreah-craze.com/.13.

14. "Star King," episode 192, 4 December 2010.

Figure 9. *Taeyeon* 태연 **singing "You Were Born to Be Loved."**[15]

Taeyeon, after all, her fans say, was born to be loved. Her fans write that she looks like an angel, that she sounds like an angel; the word "angel" hovers around her like an angel. In any case she is renowned for her emotional expression. But her emotional expression is not in the contemporary American style of emotional expression for young women performers; rather it is linked with emotional restraint, gentleness, soothing femininity, instead of being tough or cool or sexy. The restrained femininity of her tone actually makes her singing more beautiful.

In another TV singing competition between the nine members of Girls Generation, Jang Hee Young (Heeyoung), a popular idol and established vocalist of pop trio Gavy NJ (가비앤제이) sings the start of the song, "Red Lipstick" (립스틱 짙게 바르고), and the final competitor, Taeyeon,

15. https://www.youtube.com/watch?v=sOWuqEaBgII. Thanks to LoveTaeng.

must continue at that level and not trip up. It is a song that you need to be a good singer to begin with to be able to sing. This is the final sing-off of the show. Taeyeon steals it.[16]

I am aware that these are slight and rudimentary examples. In any case, Taeyeon has achieved something Whitney Houston is most famous for in the West—that is, to sing a song in a film that is better than the film.

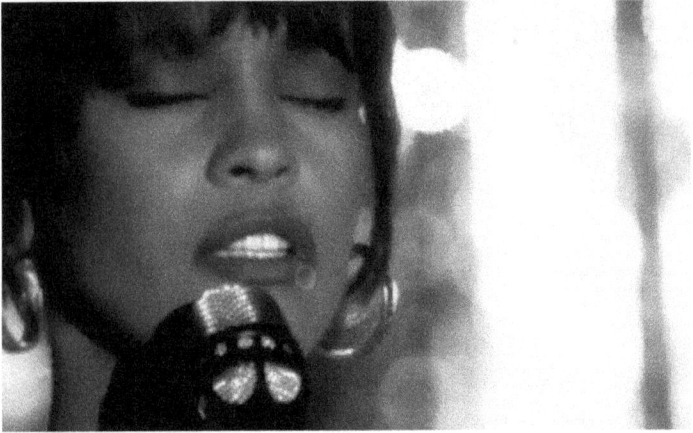

Figure 10. Whitney Houston singing "I Will Always Love You."[17]

The film *The Bodyguard* was not bad but not great, but the songs are great. This song sends shivers down the spine. Kim Taeyeon has had about *a dozen* huge hit songs that stand right out from the movies or TV dramas for which they were recorded. Like Whitney in *The Bodyguard*, Taeyeon had a huge first hit in *Hong Gil Dong* with the beautiful ballad "If" in 2008. She repeated this achievement in *The Beethoven Virus* the same year![18] But incredibly,

16. https://www.youtube.com/watch?v=faSxpZAmI3I.
17. https://www.youtube.com/watch?v=3JWTaaS7LdU.
18. Taeyeon, "If," from *Hong Gil Dong*, https://www.youtube.com/

in one movie and TV drama after another over almost a decade Taeyeon's singing has eclipsed or significantly enhanced the films in which her songs are to be heard! It is an unprecedented achievement.

In the rendition of the song "If" from 2008 (see below), Taeyeon's voice outclasses the movie, the way Whitney's did in *The Bodyguard*. The clip shows slides from the movie.[19]

I am going to go finish this chapter in the final section below by saying something about the importance of tone, so if you listen to the tracks referred to here as samples, pay attention to the *sounding* of the word, which, as they are in Korean, should you not know the language, will not distract you with their *meaning*. What I have to say about tone goes for any singer that you yourself enjoy listening to. I hope my explanation will allow you to realize why you enjoy them so much and what this has to do with soul. With the song "If," for example, the tone of Taeyeon's voice is extraordinarily soft without any effort to achieve a "soft" effect. This and the tonal range of Taeyeon's voice are exceptional. Her voice is gentle in every register, and full of longing.

---

watch?v=ncyOCEllFjs. Thanks to joshka69. "Can Your Hear Me?," from *The Beethoven Virus*, https://www.youtube.com/watch?v=gn-HNRNV9Ys. Thanks to LoveDramaOST.

19. Taeyeon, "If," from *Hong Gil Dong*, https://www.youtube.com/watch?v=ncyOCEllFjs. Thanks to joshka69.

Figure 11. "If." Still from *Hong Gil Dong.*

TONE

And so to what is most important and what this whole discourse on the opening of the Great American Song-book—and its discontinuity with the European song tradition, which achieved its height in German lieder and Italian opera—has been leading up to: the philosophy behind the soulfulness of song.

It has to do with finding harmony. The harmony is not just in the music, but in us—at least it may be in us if we seek it and if we work at it when we cannot quite find it.

The harmonic melody Wagner wrote about that I mentioned earlier is that of choral singing or orchestral music, where a number of voices in different keys, or different instruments, make the music together. *The single voice brings something new to the fore: tone.*

There is an attunement or an elective affinity between tone and soul and soulfulness. It is because of *tone* in the single voice that we can be permitted to say that song is where the soul is.

When *the word* is sung by the single voice *it is the singer's soul and intuition that speaks,* not semantics. Correspondingly, the song is received not by the cognitive faculty that grasps the semantic meaning of the words, but by the faculty of imagination. What you hear is *your emotion, not the singer's.* This is the effect of tone in a voice.

Song evokes something in us. This is an old truth. The choir boy soprano's solo voice in Allegri's *Miserere* makes one feel lifted toward heaven. That naked pure voice heard in an enormous cavernous Gothic stone church with the ceiling hundreds of feet above and acoustics like a bell with so much reverberation elate the inner being. To feel this together with a congregation is a movement of the spirit.

But still, this could be *any* young boy with the natural talent and such a trained voice. Yet with the solo voice in the era of the Great American Songbook and subsequently, the whole point is that *it could not be anyone else.* "Unforgettable" *has to be* Nat King Cole, "My Way" *has to be* Sinatra. "If" *has to be* Taeyeon.

The *event* of the Great American Song Book is in fact to have opened—or reopened in an historically new way—the *truth of tone.* This is why we love certain singers so much. When Nat King Cole sings the word "unforgettable" at the start of the song of that name, it *is* unforgettable, and the power is not in the word: the word has no power as such. It is not even in the *meaning* of the word. The soul of the song is the tone and it registers in our soul: *soul to soul.*

Words have *meaning,* but *sound* conveys an *import.* The singer's voice does not just sound or sing the words but it is the *aspect* of the sound, its tone, that conveys an *import of musical substance.* Tone is more than sound. The singer's tone has *import* you cannot put into words; if you could, there would be no point hearing the song sung by this or that particular person: you could just read the words or repeat them, or sing them yourself, or listen to any decent singer sing them. The *import of tone is the soul substance that hits the imagination in listening.* Tone is the echo of reverberation of something in us *and* in the sound. The singing voice in this regard is the supreme instrument, as has often been said. For example, Judy Garland singing "Somewhere Over the Rainbow" combines the myth of the American Dream with a perfect melody—and *perfect* here relates to a core simplicity somehow, a *lack* of fabrication so as to *lay bare*—and, most important of all in such an emotionally laden setting, the mysterious import given by Judy Garland's tone. It is her song.

The same with Taeyeon. The tone she gives the ballads she sings makes all these great hits her own. It is only when you hear some other person singing them that you realize how the song does not really belong to that other person. Consider, for example, Tori Amos singing "Somewhere Over the Rainbow"; Seohyun singing "If." This is strange, because Tori Amos and Seohyun are incontestably outstanding singers and performers, but it is a matter of the comparative import of tone.

The point is not to pay tribute to the few singers mentioned here so much as to elicit principles that explain the *bel canto* (beautiful song and beautiful singing), as Rossini called it, among the countless great performers, who are too many to mention, and to put the case that Western music came of age in Europe in the nineteenth century and the song came of age in America in the twentieth. The popular song is the real world music. The great rock and pop songs achieve transcultural and translinguistic traction and are anthemic. These anthems rise above the generation and lift its soul and unite it in the hope of a better world.

WORLD MUSIC

The question here, with world music, is could there be songs that make the world a better place? My answer is that there already are. This is already what popular music is doing in all its variety.

Ideas and words divide; religious and ideological beliefs divide the world and can tear it apart. Music brings together. Music is enjoyable. Music is a universal language precisely because it is *not* a language.

The Catholic Mass limited *melos* to a prescribed *logos*, to what could and should be said in words and thoughts, not what can be said, lyrically, or felt musically, beyond words and outside them, and beyond and outside all thinking and theology.

So music went outside the church and from the time of Haydn and Mozart developed in the nineteenth century into absolute music. At the same time Protestants also composed masses, as Bach had done already, outside the Catholic Church.

This absolute music is world music in the proper sense, for its roots are not essentially national or ethnic but inspired, that is to say, *created*, not made or made up or fabricated or thought out or engineered or according to method. Wagner, who had an orchestra twice the size of Beethoven, needed to write the material for each instrument and for its development as well as for the euphony of the whole, all the instruments sounding together simultaneously to a beautiful or powerful and evocative, moving effect. He could do it because he could hear the whole thing in his musical imagination, the creative center of his being.

So he knew what to write; there was no head scratching. No inspiration, no music. It is as simple as that.

Certainly absolute music has a history in terms of dates and nations and cities and composers and technique, but my point is precisely that world music is not reducible to these. What matters most is the *je ne sais quoi*, that quality that is discernible but that beggars explanation. Beethoven belongs to performers in China and Australia as much as to performers in its traditional heartland, in Germany and Austria. Such music is purely alive, *it is soul*, says Arthur Rubinstein, an authority.

Figure 12. Arthur Rubinstein playing the piano in Schubert's String Quintet, D. 956.[20]

At 3 minutes 41 seconds into the video Rubinstein talks of soul as we have been doing. Rubinstein's face after six minutes, when the second movement of Schubert's String Quintet, D. 956, comes in, says it all. World music such as Schubert's best music is the entrance to heaven as far as this world is concerned. And heaven is not the monopoly of any

20. https://www.youtube.com/watch?v=gexosOR7XZo.

one religion on this earth: it is beyond them all, although each of the so-called world religions undoubtedly has some narrow conduit of its own in that direction for its faithful.

Music, as we have said, has already gone ahead in this work in world music. And I mean real world music, of which the Catholic Mass is the precursor. Starting with the Great American Songbook, and actually the effect of it, the popular song became world music in the twentieth century. Pop songs are written and sung all around the world; they are not contingent on simply the language and words. What really matters in pop is the melody (which may be simple) and in particular, most importantly, the singer's unique tone, because it is *this* that brings us to life.

A good example is kirtan performer ("kirtan wallah" as he refers to himself) Krishna Das, born in New York to Jewish parents, but life-trained in an Indian ashram. The tone of his voice carries joy and sorrow simultaneously— and not just as *his* personal emotions but rather as a sensibility above and beyond him passing through him that maybe generational, transpersonal, ancestral. The listener's personal circumstance is broadened against all the world, and all directions and listeners feel the full measure of their being (which is to say their true humility) beyond personal problems, including, in some testimonies, sickness unto death. The chant, while singing names of deities in the Hindu idiom, is open to anyone. The chant is entertainment at one level—Krishna Das came through from rock music (he was in the original line-up of the heavy metal band Blue Oyster Cult)—but at another level, from the performer's point of view, kirtan is a spiritual practice, a meditation. But what matters is that the voice be able to *intone* a feeling that taps the soul of humanity, for anyone anywhere can hear it, although what exactly it *is* that they hear is beyond understanding. I am using Krishna Das here as an example of what I want to say about tone of voice and its direct power to import soulfulness through the ear into the musical receptors of our imaginations. Kirtan may not be to every reader's taste but the principle holds.

Krishna Das has never said so, and perhaps the idea has never occurred to him, but I wonder, given his Jewish background, if one can't hear generations of ancestral synagogue cantors from Old Europe in his voice—and that it is *this* import in his tone that gives his voice such power.

Krishna Das himself has explained on numerous occasions in interviews that what matters is not the music, which is like a candy coating, he says, but the repetitions of "the Names"—he prefers just "the Names" to "the Names of God," because the mention of God conjures up all sorts of misperceptions, he thinks. Kirtan is call-and-response. The singer chants the name, the congregation chants it back. It can become quite ecstatic. However, this effect is not, I would submit, merely from the repetition of the name, which would then subsume *melos* under *logos*, the religious move, the Indian move, but from the way the name is intoned, the *release* of the name from religion, the American move. This is not to discount the theurgic mystery of Divine Names and their mantric repetition, which however must remain a mystery, and which Krishna Das often refers to when he talks about the names as *mantras*; but I refer to a natural *gift* of vocal tonality. So I am saying it is not the music as such, and it is not the name of the deity as such, but it is *the way it is sung.* There are many kirtan singers but none of them sing the names the way Krishna Das sings them. The music is the same, the names are the same for all the kirtan singers, but the way Krishna Das sings the names is absolutely inimitable and unique and *the way* he sings them is what attracts people, even people who are hurting badly inside and are even at death's door, and makes them testify to the healing effect of listening and participating with his chant, and has made him something of a "celebrity" kirtan singer.

So to repeat what we have said above, when *the word* is sung by the single voice *it is the singer's soul and intuition that speaks*, not semantics. Correspondingly, the song is received not by the cognitive faculty that grasps the semantic meaning of the words, but by the faculty of imagination. Therefore, with the example of Krishna Das, it does not matter what the words *mean*, he has said no-one knows, the names are too old, so we, the participants in his kirtan, do not need do know anything about Hindu deities or religion. What we hear is *our emotion, not his*. What we are moved by in listening is a deeper part of ourselves, not him. This is the effect of tone in a voice.

Possibly, more speculatively, when we listen *deeply* to this kind of music we attune not just to the singer's meditation, but his (or her) teacher's, and of course his (or her) teacher would say the same. So what we hear is the *transmission* of something archaic. Something from the wild earth. Something Adamic, as the Kabbalah would put it.

A parallel example to what we are talking about from contemporary Christianity is referred to by Darlene Zschech, the former longtime worship leader of what has become the world's most widespread and leading Pentecostal church, Hillsong, based in Sydney. Zschech says about the power of song:

> Well, a song's amazing, because you're streaming all our crazy thoughts, into a purposed and intentional few lines that you actually get to announce and declare. It's a song of faith. It's not just a musical expression. It's a song of faith every time.
>
> So if you are announcing that God is here with us, and that he is here in the storm and in the trial, that is SO incredible, that you get to be

part of bringing a concise declaration that helps lift people out of the mud.[21]

Worship leading requires the worship leader to impart *enthusiasm*. The word "enthusiasm" comes from the Greek, *en-theos*, meaning to be possessed or inspired by the god. In this case Jesus is the god. To make declarations and announcements of faith in a worship atmosphere that are going to catch on with the multitude of people and thereby "bring people to Christ," as they say, requires the right music. Here the song writing of U2 has been perhaps more crucial than any in showing how to build a song emotionally. One has to think only of their songs "In the Name of Love" or "All I Want Is You." U2's music has opened up an *emotional space* that virtually the entirety of Christian rock music inhabits. Emotion is harnessed in the slow build-up to dramatic crescendo in which there are strong affirmations, and the music gains traction from the very *simplicity* and repetitive predictability that is so heavily criticized by popular philosophers of music like Roger Scruton. These are the kind of emotional songs that attempt to be anthemic or to have an anthemic "feel." Bono says exactly the same as Krishna Das despite all the difference between them: "I try to get to the place where I am not singing the song, the song is singing me."[22] These are the great songs (no matter who is singing) that sing us when we sing along. These Christian worship songs are world music. Worship music is principally what has been building the new age churches throughout Europe and America, Africa and Asia. Hillsong's story alone, in this regard, is quite astonishing.[23]

21. Teagan Russell, "Darlene," *Eternity* (August 2017): 8, www.eternitynews.com.au.

22. https://www.youtube.com/watch?v=LD4Bm-X3148.

23. *Let Hope Rise*. http://hillsongmovie.com/.

I have mentioned two conspicuous examples of impartation of tone doing something to us and activating the world; but more broadly, at concerts, whether large or small, something of the same happens. Songs bring people together and unite them.[24] This is the result of *initiation* of the senses.

The expansiveness of this sounding, which we have recognized as distinctively culturally American, beyond particular religion or nationality or ethnicity, breathing out and through these "barriers," is properly ecumenical and inter-religious. It is a foretaste of music to come, and perhaps of suitable festivals and rituals corresponding with such music and relating to our planetary sensibility, if we can find one, as Wagner first envisaged with his Bayreuth but which since then music festivals everywhere—as well as the leading churches throughout the Christian world—embrace. And the ecological and earth sensibility of American poets like Gary Snyder and Wendell Berry *lead the way* back for those of us in places where this sensibility is lost and forgotten.

Here, with world music, we have a glimpse of harmony. Peace among people (finding harmony) requires religion and nonreligion to release *melos* beyond *logos*. But beyond absolute music where this has already happened, for the first time ever in the nineteenth century in Europe, it requires, as the American popular song shows, the human voice to be heard and beauty to be released on the breath of the hallowed word, which is the human word, above all, *love*, the main subject of song and resonance of soul.

---

24. https://www.youtube.com/watch?v=o4wofd-rZtE   Robbie Williams singing "Angels" live at Knebworth. His three shows attracted 375,000 fans and that night traffic was completely jammed up within a 50 mile radius of the event. https://www.youtube.com/watch?v=45A6R9L7T04 Adele live at the Royal Albert Hall, London. Wait until the audience take over and sing it

Bibliography

Abram, David. *The Spell of the Sensuous.* New York: Vintage, 1997.

Barenboim, Daniel. *Everything Is Connected: The Power of Music.* London: Weidenfeld and Nicolson, 2008.

Baudrillard, Jean. *America.* London: Verso, 2010.

———. *The Transparency of Evil: Essays on Extreme Phenomena.* Translated by James Benedict. London: Verso, 1993.

Berry, Thomas. *The Dream of the Earth.* San Francisco: Sierra Club, 1988.

Berry, Wendell. *This Day: Sabbath Poems* 1979–2013. Berkeley, CA: Counterpoint 2013.

Del Nevo, Matthew. *Art Music: Love, Listening, Soulfulness.* New York: Routledge, 2017.

———. *The Valley Way of Soul: Melancholy, Poetry and Soulmaking.* Strathfield, NSW: St. Pauls, 2008.

———. *The Work of Enchantment.* New Brunswick: Transaction, 2011.

François de Sales. *Traité de l'amour de Dieu.* 2 volumes. Paris: Seuil, 1996.

Hegel, G. W. F., *The Phenomenology of Spirit.* Translated by A. V. Miller. Oxford: Oxford University Press, 1977.

Kant, Immanuel. *Critique of Judgment.* Translated by Werner S. Pluhar. Indianapolis: Hackett, 1987.

Kierkegaard, Søren. *Sickness Unto Death.* Translated by Alastair Hannay. London: Penguin, 1989.

Küng, Hans. *The Incarnation of God: An Introduction to Hegel's Theological Thought as a Prolegomena to a Future Christology.* Translated by J. R. Stephenson. New York: Crossroad, 1987.

Langer, Susanne K., ed. *Reflections on Art: A Source Book of Writings by Artists, Critics & Philosophers.* New York: Oxford University Press, 1961.

Merton, Thomas. *The Asian Journal of Thomas Merton.* Edited by Naomi Burton, Patrick Hart, and James Laughlin. London: Sheldon, 1974.

Nhat Hanh, Thich. *Old Path, White Clouds.* Berkeley: Parallax, 1991.

Ranson, David. *Across the Great Divide: Bridging Spirituality and Religion Today.* Sydney: St. Pauls, 2002.

Rilke, Rainer Maria. *The Notebook of Malte Laurids Brigge.* Translated by John Linton. London: Hogarth, 1959.

Sacks, Jonathan, *The Home We Build Together: Recreating Society.* London: Continuum, 2007.

Schopenhauer, Arthur. *The World as Will and Representation.* Translated by E. F. J. Payne. 2 volumes. New York: Dover, 1969.

Snyder, Gary. *Earth House Hold.* New York: New Directions, 1969.

———. *The Practice of the Wild.* San Francisco: Northpoint, 1990.

Teilhard de Chardin, Pierre. *Hymn of the Universe.* London: Collins, 1965.

Trungpa, Chögyam. *Cutting Through Spiritual Materialism.* Boston: Shambhala, 2002.

Wagner, Richard. *The Artwork of the Future.* Translated by Emma Warner. London: London Wagner Society, 2013. A special issue of the *Wagner Journal.*

———. *Beethoven, with a Supplement from the Philosophical Works of Arthur Schopenhauer.* Translated by Edward Danreuther. London: William Reeves, 1880.

Index